APPLIED
ASTROLOGY

APPLIED ASTROLOGY

COMPANION BOOK
TO
THE MODERN TEXT-BOOK OF ASTROLOGY

by

MARGARET E. HONE
D.F.Astrol.S.

Vice-President of the Astrological Lodge of London
Vice-Principal of the Faculty of Astrological Studies
Author of *The Modern Text-Book of Astrology*

L. N. FOWLER & CO. LTD.
1201–1203 HIGH ROAD
CHADWELL HEATH, ROMFORD, ESSEX RM6 4DH

This book is dedicated to

ALL STUDENTS OF THE FACULTY OF ASTROLOGICAL STUDIES, PAST AND PRESENT

with whom so many happy hours have been spent
both personally and postally ;

also to

FUTURE STUDENTS

who will carry on the work

First edition, February 1953
First impression, August 1962
Second impression, December 1966
Third impression, October 1968
Fourth impression, November 1970
Fifth impression, November 1972
Sixth impression, December 1974
Seventh impression, December 1977
Eighth impression, August 1979
Ninth impression, May 1983

SBN 85243 073 6

Printed and bound in Great Britain at
The Camelot Press Ltd, Southampton

CONTENTS

Charts by
WILLIAM G. KINGSWELL

v

FOREWORD

A book such as this has long been needed. The older generation of students will recall that excellent case-delineations of interesting subjects, carefully annotated, used to appear in *Modern Astrology* and were certainly very helpful to the young students of those days. These might well have been—but never were—collected into book-form, and thus beginners were forced to learn the hard way which in some instances produces excellent results, but not always. Few students are so gifted as not to benefit from a helping hand.

Mrs. Hone has the immense advantage of a number of years of practical experience, as a well-known and busy professional consultant, and also as a teacher, both private and as the mainspring of the activities of the Faculty of Astrological Studies. It will be seen from a perusal of this work that she has evolved a compact method of analysis and a carefully thought out plan of exposition. But, good though these are, she has wisely stressed the desirability of each practitioner carefully developing his own ideas and special ways of presentation. For Astrology treats of living things, and no hard-and-fast system could ever be finally satisfactory.

However, it may be extremely useful as a platform from which to start ; and those who study this book and carry out its precepts are likely to reach a high standard of work far more quickly than those who have no such guidance. In fact, if they conscientiously and carefully study the Author's methods, they can scarcely fail to produce excellent results. If they are naturally endowed with an interest in human nature and a genuine desire to help mankind, so much the better. That is a *sine qua non* for all who aspire to be really good professional astrologers.

By showing each map according to Placidus as well as by the *modus aequalis* Mrs. Hone demonstrates her fairmindedness and gives each student an opportunity to compare these two methods without difficulty ; and if some students may be inclined to complain of the confusion existing in astrological circles on this subject, one can but reply that this is no fault of the writer, whose personal preference for equal houses, taken from the ascendant along the ecliptic, is well known.

The Faculty of Astrological Studies has already done much to raise the standards of professional astrological work in Great Britain—and indeed in a number of other parts of the world—and it will now have a further weapon in its armoury wherewith to fight careless analysis and slovenly presentation.

CHARLES E. O. CARTER.

July, 1953.

INTRODUCTION

After many years of teaching astrology, first to private pupils and then to classes, it has become increasingly obvious that the student is hampered in his early days by not being able to see examples of work set out and arranged by a working astrologer. It is hoped that this book will help to fill the need especially for those abroad, unable to attend lectures. Other astrologers may not agree with the interpretations as given but even in this case, clarification of ideas may result through the presentation of these examples for discussion.

Grateful acknowledgment is now made, firstly to those who have so freely given permission for their personal letters and chart-interpretations to be published ; secondly to those who have helped to correct the book ; Miss Jacinthe Buddicom, who has acted as checker of significators and Mr. J. M. Filbey, who calculated the charts.

As it is difficult to write a detailed book without mistakes, these are apologised for in advance.

MARGARET E. HONE.

London, 1953.

CHAPTER 1

" BACKWARDS " AND " FORWARDS " ASTROLOGY

THE two simple words quoted in the title of this chapter have found a place of their own in describing astrological interpretation. The one is used for work done *backwards to* a chart when all the character traits and events in a life are first known through reading a biography written by a trained author who has carefully collected all available details about the subject of his book.

The other is used for work done *forwards from* a chart, using astrological technique to deduce from it the character traits and also the tendencies which may eventuate in happenings *of a certain nature* in a life, this being very different from prediction of actual occurences.

All students have access to examples of *backwards astrology* both in text-books and in lectures in which charts of well-known people are discussed ; certain signs, planetary placings and aspects are found to agree with outstanding characteristics as previously described ; progressed positions by one of the customary methods are found to correlate with events which are known to have occurred at given dates.

It is extremely valuable for a learner to study these and to give himself a similar exercise, but *he is not using his deductive ability which he must strengthen if he is to become an able astrologer.* He is rarely able to read examples of *forwards astrology* exactly as written to a client by an astrologer who has had to think out the interpretation of the chart in question for himself, sometimes after an interview with the person concerned, sometimes with only a case-history arrived at through correspondence.

As in all professions, practitioners develop their own ideas, first according to traditional teaching, then according to contemporary changes of opinion and lastly according to their own experience. It is not to be expected that any two would completely agree in their interpretation of a chart, nor would any two use similar phraseology in clothing the ideas they wish to express, but modern methods of teaching have shown that a dozen students working separately on a chart of a person unknown to them, for home-work or in an examination, *will all produce similar descriptions* (reasonably correct in the estimation of the tutor to whom the person is known), thus showing that the technique is valid, whoever may use it.

Most of the examples in the chapters which follow are of the latter category. It is hoped that students who agree with the methods used will be helped by them in their own work and that discussion will be stimulated amongst those who do not.

CHAPTER 2

INTERPRETATION DISCUSSED FOR THE INTERESTED INQUIRER

The Work of an Astrologer

THE work of an astrologer is the use of technique and experience in the elucidation of the meaning of temporary positions of the moving objects in the celestial sphere, in relation to the embodiment of that meaning in the lives of any created things, starting at any temporal moment, on the terrestrial sphere.

To do this work he must first understand, as far as this is possible, *the ever-changing nature of moments of time*. The relationship between Sun and Earth forever takes place in the plane of the ecliptic. This is the plane of relationship of the Sun with everything of which it is the centre. Without the Sun there is no light, no warmth, no life, no power, no vitality, no creativity. In modern days, this great truth is forgotten because of the mechanical use of oil, gas and electricity for light and warmth and power, generally without a thought for the source from which their energy starts. Mechanical clocks are used to show the passing of the hours of a day. The average man in the street could not explain the astronomical basis on which the working of these is arranged.

Even so, it is a fact that there is nothing on the terrestrial sphere, neither animal, vegetable nor mineral, which was not originally an integral part of the fabric of that sphere.

Without the Earth-Sun relationship which constitutes the plane of the ecliptic, the " dust " of the Earth could not embody life which continues to re-create itself, nor could the life so embodied develop mind, which continues the work of creativity in ways such as those of art, literature and commerce.

This great main principle has been recognised and revered from time immemorial. It seems to have been the core of the earliest religions in the world's history.

The Greeks gave the name " planets " to all moving bodies in the sky including the Sun and Moon. In astrological practice, the same habit continues. The Moon and the planets pass on to the Earth what they receive from the central Sun.

Thus, astrologically, the Sun is held to generate the most powerful, vivifying principle of life, while the lesser bodies correlate with subsidiary principles.

Since the inhabitants of Earth can interpret these principles only in relation to one moving body, namely that on which they live, the positions of the other bodies, calculated from tables astronomically determined, must be stated as in that relation. Hence, though the Sun is the centre of the Solar system, astrologers, like navigators, express relationships geocentrically.

The Method of an Astrologer

Having made a circle of the usual 360 degrees to represent the ecliptic, the degrees on the horizon and meridian at a certain place at a certain time are marked. The symbols for the planets are inserted beside the degrees which they occupy. So far, the work is astronomically accurate.

Other insertions are then made according to one or other of several controversial and conflicting astrological theories. By these, the astrological " houses " are arranged. Discussion of the differences between them is the province of a text-book, so this will not now be included.*

With modern Tables and chart-forms, this operation of charting can be performed in a very few minutes. By reference to text-books, the rudiments of interpretation can be learnt. The student can then, in the mediæval phrase, " delineate a horoscope," but he cannot yet deserve the name of *astrologer*, any more than the opener of a few tins of food is worthy to be called cook.

Interpretation of a Chart

The word " delineation " is unfamiliar to the public and the word " horoscope " has been applied journalistically to astrologically phrased remarks general to all whose birth-days fall within periods of thirty days or so.

It is therefore better to think of *interpretation of an astronomically determined chart by the use of astrological technique*, and to remember always that one is not merely interpreting a paper chart, but is acknowledging the sublime truth of the ecliptical relationship of the Sun, Moon and planets to the Earth and all that in it is.

Two basic concepts of this technique are :—

(*a*)   That the inter-relationships of the pattern so formed at the first moment of existence of any person or thing can be interpreted in terms explanatory of that person or thing.

(*b*)   That charts of further time-sequences relative to this initial moment can be interpreted to give an idea of *trends* to take place in the life of the thing, enterprise or person as it develops.

With knowledge of the general environment of the thing or person in question, happenings in accord with the *nature of such trends* can be postulated.

The astrological worker can no more be certain of these results than the doctor who prognoses the course of disease in a patient, but he can speak of *likely trends*.

Spare-time Interest, Practice or Research

This technique can be used for interest's sake by those who are keen students of life and like to be aware of the underlying astronomical pattern beneath outward behaviour of people and of events.

It can also be used by a capable practitioner to help others to understand themselves, and to find their way more easily through the perplexities of life.

Experienced workers can devote themselves to research on this subject. In all fields of inquiry, advance is made almost invariably by such work, usually financed by public funds. Astrologers have had no such aid, thus being without published findings to help them in their desire to improve their technique.

Preparation for Work

In order to become an astrologer, a student must perfect himself in his technique and apply himself to gaining experience. These two objects are gained by familiarising himself with *the essential natures* of the planets in their manifold ecliptical relationships, and by watching these in their embodiment in the lives of people, in businesses, and in political and world events.

His results are obtained empirically. They are not easy to classify. Statistical evaluation

* See *The Modern Text-book of Astrology*, chapters 7 and 16, by M. E. Hone.

inclines to falsify their truth rather than to prove it, since the factors used in astrological work are not repetitive in all details, so cannot be fully compared from time to time.

Modern scientific practice demands that the truth of a theory shall, if possible, be proved by repeated experiments, each carried out exactly as the others before it. No such experimentation can be made in astrological work since the astronomical factors are constantly changing. The Earth-Sun relationship varies momentarily. As the planets move in their orbits according to their different speeds, their angular relationships to Earth and to each other change. Therefore when any one configuration repeats, other factors will have come into the picture, causing modification of the deductions drawn about the main matter under consideration. It is therefore better to state definitely to those who cannot believe anything without such *proof* that this cannot be brought forward. To those who realise this, it can, however, be stated that strong *evidence* can be examined by those who have taken the trouble to learn the a-b-c of the technique so that the significance of such evidence can be understood by them.

Application

To no one but an artist himself would a knowledge of the technique of painting be of any value, if he refused to apply it. Usually he is ready to do this in order to give pleasure or comfort to all who like his type of expression, to cause argument amongst those who do not and, in these days of economic struggle when artists are no more kept in comfort by the nobility, he does it to provide a necessary income in return for his work.

The astrologer must also apply his technique if he is to achieve these same ends. He can specialise in many forms of his art, according to his other abilities. If he is a clever journalist and has an interest in world affairs, he will specialise in applying his interpretative technique to charts of world events and of leaders prominent in the affairs of countries. The practice of this is technically called *mundane* or *political astrology*.

If he is interested in human nature, he will specialise in interpretation of charts of people. This is what has been known as *horoscopic delineation*. The present writer prefers to call it *astro-analysis*. Like a doctor or a weather forecaster, both will make their diagnoses and prognoses. The specialist in *personal astrology* will study charts of the beginnings of people, of moments when relationships begin between people such as first meetings, decisions to form partnerships, to start societies, to marry, to go into business and so on.

The examples given in this book are chosen both to interest the non-astrological inquirer and to help the astrological student, though it is not to be expected that the former will be able to understand the technical references and paragraphs of astrological discussion.

CHAPTER 3

INTERPRETATION DISCUSSED FOR THE STUDENT OF ASTROLOGY

INTERPRETATION of a natal map is for the purpose of showing to the person concerned just what the astronomical *pattern in the sky* at his birth moment means as his *pattern for life.* Interpretation of further time sequences in relation to this chart, by any of the different methods of progressions, directions, or transits, is to show the person that happenings, psychological, physical or in the sphere of outward events, are correlative with such sequences ; moreover that such happenings in the past have been *of the nature* of the planets involved and in accordance with what would have been thought likely from an understanding study of the pattern of the birth moment. It is therefore considered to be likely that present circumstances can be understood by a study of present sequences and future probabilities may be anticipated by a study of sequences which can be calculated for future years.

Since every interpreter must work after the manner of his own life pattern, no two will work alike, varying in interpretation from the same birth data. In the same way, a group of artists painting the same scene will produce a collection of different pictures, yet all recognisable as the same subject.

So no hard and fast rules can be given for interpretation but general suggestions can be made and examples given from which students can learn while evolving their own style.

Suggestions to Students for Consideration in Interpretation of Personal Charts

1. Think of your client before yourself.

2. If he is coming to you for consultation, ask yourself *why* he is coming and in what way he really needs help. If he begins by concealing this, explain to him that he would not go to a doctor and demand a diagnosis and a cure, while concealing his symptoms and the conditions surrounding him in which he had to work out his cure. In the rare cases when a client persists in withholding his " symptoms," it is better to explain to him that you are an astrological practitioner and not a fortune-teller and to say that you would prefer not to interest yourself in his case any further.

3. It is better to have a certain amount of case-history beforehand so that you can concentrate on the problem presented rather than be forced to make generalisations.

4. The astronomical pattern of the client's birth-moment should be charted *in detail* before the appointment is kept. Your astrological notes should be *fully made.*

5. Make notes on a few past years. This can be done (*a*) retrospectively, that is, by listing astrological factors to events previously given by him, or (*b*) deductively, that is, by noting certain years outstanding for major configurations either by secondary progressions, methods such as the One-Degree measure, or by transits and so on, giving an interpretation of the *type of event* likely to have happened in those years. *Never* is it wise to try to gain credit for yourself by being too exact in detailing such events. This is stretching deductive ability too far and can bring discredit on yourself and on the art of which you have taken the responsibility of being the representative.

By the latter means, you can make changes in the degrees on the angles of the chart, hoping to get the given birth moment nearer to exactitude. (The word " rectify " is deliberately avoided, as it has been over-used to describe the *changing* of times given approximately for birth moments. In most cases when these are " right-ified," no records exist to prove the experimenter right or wrong. When such records are found, the " right-ification " is so often proved to be " wrong-ification " that it would appear safer not to give too much credence to claims of astrological workers in this respect.

If the correlation of past configurations with past events proves to be correct, some evidence is then available to show that work on future possibilities may be reliable.

6. Having established confidence between your client and yourself, your work is to explain his unconscious motivations to him so that he begins to see that he thinks and behaves and also reacts to the behaviour of others, not so much because of any of the motives that his more critical friends project on to him, *but because he is an embodiment of a life pattern which is inherent in ecliptical relationships at his birth, this being there whether he is aware of it or not.*

7. Get him to state his problem in the most clear manner possible. This will be his first step towards resolving it. While he talks, mark in your notes the phrases *which you have written beforehand*, which he now brings out of his own unconsciousness. Later on, you will show him these to let him observe the truth of deduction by the technique of " forwards " astrology which you are using. Listen quietly, giving him the opportunity for what Jung calls " a clearing of a cramp in the unconscious." During this time, and especially in the first few moments, he will speak his map to you, using every turn of speech and mannerism and characterisation which you have already noted as to be expected from the charted pattern. Note these ; compare them with what you have already written ; later on show him the correlation.

8. Having found out the real problem about which he has come to you, concentrate on that one point and give all the help you can from all data at your disposal.

9. Try to plan your day so that you write up a short report on the interview as soon as possible while you are still within that field of *rapport* that has grown around you both.

10. You must now suit your written report to your client and his needs. While being yourself, yet think first of him. You cannot write to a clergyman as to a stockbroker nor to a young girl as to an experienced woman.

11. Reconsider your skeleton notes in the light of what has passed between you. Ask yourself the following questions :—

(a) Have I made a proper *synthesis* of the outstanding factors of the chart, not stressing one factor more than another or failing to see that one will modify or intensify another ?

(b) Have I considered the actual *principles of the planets*, working, as I know by my technique, differently through the *signs* they are now in, and in the departments of life in which they are placed by *house* ? *

(c) Have I considered the modifications imposed by the *combination of aspects* to some planets as charted, and the *lack of aspects* to others ?

(d) Have I thought out the difference between the *innate inclination of the outer self-expression of this life* as shown by the sign containing the nonagesimal,† and the conditioning of the ruler of that sign, in relation to the *life experience* probable to that person according to the sign containing the M.C.‡ and the conditioning

---

* House position must vary according to house system used. Discussion on this point is not the function of this book. For full discussion see *The Modern Text-book of Astrology*, by the same author.

† Cusp of 10th house by Equal House system of house division.

‡ Cusp of 10th house by Quadrant systems of house division. See Chapter 13.

of its ruler ? Have I allowed for the conflict between these two, or noted the happy lack of conflict ?

(*e*)   Have I remembered that some aspects are very common and that the planets concerned can make no others ? (Aspects between Sun and Mercury and Venus.) Have I realised that some aspects are common to all born within a certain period ? (Aspects between heavy planets remaining within orbs for days and even weeks and recurring through retrogradation.)

(*f*)   Have I considered the present situation from every possible angle of current progressions and transits in the light of the *nature of the planets* not as an isolated circumstance but *in relation to the natal map* ? For instance, conjunction of Jupiter by transit with an important planet in a natal chart will mean *expansion* (keyword meaning). Is the life pattern that of a rash, impetuous, enthusiastic, optimistic, outgoing person in whom expansion will mean *exaggeration* of these qualities so that he may need a cautionary word ? Or is it that of a cautious, reserved, timid, hesitant type to whom expansion may mean added *opportunity* so that he may need a word of encouragement to go ahead at just this time ?

Notes on Acknowledgment of Sources of Included Remarks

1. *Philosophies and Beliefs*

While it is natural that all will word interpretations in the light of their own philosophy of life, it would be well to give due acknowledgment to the sources of those doctrines which are not essentially astrological. As an example, the theory of reincarnation is widely held by many astrologers who take it that character traits are " brought over " from another life. While this may be acceptable to some readers of interpretations, it would be quite unacceptable to others.

In any case, astrology is a technique by which an interpretation is attempted according to the astronomical sky-pattern at a given moment. It is for all the world and not for any particular sect or doctrine with its special beliefs.

2. *Writings of Others*

In days gone by, interpretation was often taught by means of constant reference to paragraphs about planets, signs, houses and aspects in standard works by well-known authors. The result was that character readings often contained paragraphs copied entirely from such books. The method of interpretation brought forward by the present writer is based on deduction from what is known of the *natures* of the planets, with their modifications through sign, house and aspect. Even so, it may often be helpful to quote from the books of authors whose work is of great value. Such a source should *always* be acknowledged.

3. *Deductions from Non-astrological Sources*

Occasionally, birth-times are given as having been obtained by spirit communication ; astrologers versed in the techniques of hand-reading or numerology may form deductions through these techniques ; others may wish to include some of the varied and conflicting " meanings " for zodiacal degrees* obtained by clairvoyance and published as such in certain books. The source of these should be clearly stated and defined as non-astrological.

* Students should be careful to differentiate between these and suggestions as to significances attached to certain *areas* of the zodiac, arrived at by careful study of charts by C. E. O. Carter in his book, *An Encyclopædia of Psychological Astrology*. There may be reasons for these such as the proximity of certain fixed stars or other astronomical features not yet understood, for instance, those about which we are now hearing, found by the new technique of radio-astronomy.

Extract from the Code of Ethics of the Faculty of Astrological Studies

This Code was written in 1952 by the Principal, Charles E. O. Carter. Every student is asked to abide by it and none may obtain the Diploma of the Faculty unless willing to sign an agreement to do so. In reference to the preceding paragraphs, two sections of this are now quoted, since their careful wording will commend them to all students.

2.   (c)   I will in every case make an original and individual study of the case before me and will not use any form of reduplication, nor will I use in my work extracts from others' writings without due acknowledgment.

      (d)   In work stated to be astrological I will not insert anything that is not founded upon true astrological science. Should I desire to impart advice or information derived from other sources I will write this upon a separate sheet with an express statement that it is not based upon Astrology.

CHAPTER 4

METHOD IN INTERPRETATION

THE examples of interpretation which follow have been chosen to give as much variety as possible and to show the usual work of a practising astrologer. No consideration is given to a type of work in which pre-fabricated descriptions of signs as Ascendants, or of Sun, Moon and planets in signs, houses and so on, are clipped together with no attempt at synthesis or with but a final general paragraph. In these examples, each interpretation is written, as a whole, for each client.

System of Interpretation

The method used is that evolved by the writer and given in detail in *The Modern Text-book of Astrology.*

In brief, a few keywords giving a central core of meaning are suggested for each *planet, sign* and *house*, being modified by *aspects* between them. Students are trained to avoid all guesswork and to make a beginning by a literal, if stilted, *translation* of a chart, factor by factor, and always in the same order. These stilted phrases are then remodelled into suitable sentences. To each phrase, a marginal note is added as to the *category* under which it may be placed. Interpretation is then made by collecting all sentences which come under the first category with which to begin the writing of the analysis, synthesising them into a rounded whole.

The same is done with the remaining categories, stressing those important in the work on hand, giving short mention to or entirely omitting those not applicable.

Some interpretations which follow are prefaced by full notes in order to help students. Whether these are included or not, in each piece of work the keyword system has been used, but without any desire to claim it as the best or only method. Other ways will appeal to other workers according to their own life-patterns. What is necessary is that there should be a clear-cut path for the student to follow until such a time as he can plan a way for himself.

Acknowledgment has been made in the Introduction to all those whose kindness has made it possible to reproduce, under fictitious names, analyses done for them recently, but in case the reader has not read this, it should be repeated that *full permission has been given to use all material which follows* in the hope that this may help others in their studies.

Except for minor editing, *no alteration has been made in what was originally written in course of practice. The aim has been to reflect the everyday work of an astrological consultant.* It will be noted that no astrological phraseology is used in writing to those who do not understand it but marginal references to all significators are entered, using the symbols which are the " short-hand " of astrology. These never appear on the copy sent to the client but are entered into the margin of the carbon copy filed by the consultant, ready for reference at any time when the analysis is again needed, such as a time of difficulty in the future when the client again feels that astrological help can strengthen his hand.

CHAPTER 5

SYNOPSIS OF THE KEYWORD SYSTEM AND EXAMPLES OF INTERPRETATION

The Planets and their Principles

Keywords :—

Sun	Power ; Vitality ; Self-expression.
Moon	Response ; Fluctuation.
Mercury	Communication (mentally and by transport).
Venus	Harmony ; Unison ; Relatedness.
Mars	Energy ; Heat ; Activation.
Jupiter	Expansion ; Preservation.
Saturn	Limitation ; Cold.
Uranus	Change (Revolutionary ; Disruptive ; Dictatorial).
Neptune	Nebulousness ; Impressionability.
Pluto	Elimination ; Renewal ; Regeneration.

The Signs as Customarily Grouped

(a) *The Triplicities*

Keywords :—

Fire	Ardent ; Keen.
Earth	Practical ; Cautious.
Air	Intellectual ; Communicative.
Water	Emotional ; Unstable ; Sensitive.

(b) *The Quadruplicities*

Keywords :—

Cardinal	Outgoing.
Fixed	Resistant to change.
Mutable	Adaptable.

(c) *Positivity and Negativity*

Keywords :—

Positive	Self-expressive.
Negative	Self-repressive, receptive.

The Signs and their Modes of Planetary Expression

A planet in a sign will show its own principle, urge or drive, but it will do so in the mode of that sign.

Keywords :—

In Aries	Assertively.
Taurus	Possessively.
Gemini	Communicatively, with alert versatility.

Cancer	Sensitively, protectively.
Leo	Creatively, joyfully.
Virgo	Critically, detailedly.
Libra	Harmoniously, unitedly.
Scorpio	Passionately, secretively, penetratingly.
Sagittarius	Widely, deeply, free-ranging.
Capricorn	Prudently, coolly, aspiringly.
Aquarius	Detachedly, scientifically.
Pisces	With appreciation of the intangibles, often confusedly.

The Houses and their Meanings

A planet in a house will show its own principle, urge or drive according to the sphere of activity of that house.

Keywords :—

1–6 Personal

1. The person.
2. Possessions and feelings of the person.
3. Short communications. Mental interests. Nearest relations such as brothers and sisters. Neighbours.
4. Home (Base).
5. Creativity, risks, pleasures, love, children.
6. Service ; in work, in health.

7–12 Wider Expression

7. Others in close connection.
8. Possessions of or from others. Legacies, shared feelings. Life-force in birth, sex, death and after-life.
9. Longer communications. More profound mental interests.
10. Matters outside the home. Public standing. Attainment.
11. More detached contacts such as friendships. Objectives.
12. More secluded service. Retirement ; escape, sacrifice ; hidden life of the unconscious.

(The two sets of houses are arranged in parallel columns so that it may be observed that there is an extension of expression from each in the first six to that one which is connected to it by polarity in the other six.)

Interpretation of Planet in Sign and House

Refer to Keywords. Put their meanings together in what will be stilted language. Change into conversational words.

Example 1.—Sun in Aries in 9th house.

By keywords :—" Your *power* and *vitality* are used *assertively* in matters of *travel* and *deeper study*."

By interpretation :—" You are a busy, forceful, energetic person, keen to get about, see other countries and use your brain for serious study."

Example 2.—Uranus in Aquarius in 7th house.

By keywords :—" Your urge to be *disruptive* is used *detachedly* when dealing with others in *close connection*."

By interpretation :—" You have a strong tendency to split from anyone with whom you have placed yourself intimately, either in marriage or in business. You will do this coolly and in an independent spirit."

The Aspects

The interpretation so found will be modified by Aspects

Name	Implication
Conjunction	Strength of meaning (according to nature of planets).
Opposition	Tenseness.
Trine	Ease of working.
Square	Difficulty of working but can be energising and constructive.
Sextile	As trine but weaker.
Semi-square	Difficulty.
Sesquiquadrate (Square plus half a square)	Difficulty.
Quincunx	Strain.
Semi-sextile	Lack of ease.

Suggested Categories under which to Collect Notes

Abbreviation	Category	Refer also to :—
Char.	1. General Characteristics	1st house. Sun and Moon in full detail. Anything outstanding in general formation.
Ment.	2. Mentality, creativity, Intuitional ability	3rd and 9th mental trends. 5th creativity, 8th and 12th intuitional ability. Mercury and other planets for special abilities.*
Car.	3. Career, money, working ability	10th career, with all general tendencies. 6th work and ability for it. Contrasted strengths of Jupiter and Saturn for success and obstacles to overcome. 7th for partners and associates. 2nd and 8th for money.
Sp. time	4. Spare time occupations	1st general. 5th pleasures. Sun and Moon and ruler general indications.
Friends Love Marr.	5. Personal contacts Friends, attachments Marriage	11th friends, 5th love, 7th marriage, 8th sexual love. Venus for ability for *rapport*. Sun in woman's map. Moon in man's. Mars for out-reaching force.
Fam.	6. Family contacts	4th and 10th mother and father, also Moon and Saturn. 3rd brothers and sisters, also Mercury. 5th children.
Health	7. Health	1st type of person. 6th health. 12th sometimes hospitalisation. Sun vitality and heart. Moon functional disorders. Saturn chills, falls. Mars burns, scalds, cuts, fevers. Jupiter liver trouble. Uranus circulation, also breaks, sprains.
Trav.	8. Travel	3rd and 9th, Mercury and Jupiter.

It is not to be expected that every detail of a chart can be included in an interpretation. The notes of the categories must be read and a *good, interesting synthesis* of all under that heading must be made. Each must be taken in turn in the same way, until all is welded into one whole.

* See Chapter 3, *The Modern Text-book*.

CHAPTER 6

ASTRO-ANALYSIS FOR A CLIENT UNACQUAINTED WITH ASTROLOGICAL TERMINOLOGY

Chart A.—A PSYCHOLOGICAL STUDY OF A VICAR.

Reasons for Inclusion

THIS chart has been chosen for inclusion, and also for first place in the series, because it is a good example of what an astrological consultant may have to deal with.

Full notes, on which the interpretation is based, are included so that the reader may become familiar with this methodical manner of working. (These will be found for Chart B also, but not afterwards since they would increase the size of the book unduly.)

An astrologer cannot always work with his client by means of an interview. He may be prevented by reason of distance. There are some astrologers who prefer to work without seeing their clients. These are often of the intuitive type with water signs and houses well emphasised in their charts. They prefer to allow their intuition to work and give importance to what they " feel " from the chart which they are studying. Others have no facilities for interviewing even if they would prefer this method. All must work in the way which suits them best.

If an interview is not possible, a full case-history should be requested by letter with definite statement of the particular problems to be considered or the reasons for having the work done.

From reading of text-books and attendance at lectures at which backwards astrology is the rule rather than the exception, inexperienced learners are apt to think that work done by astrological technique is easy and always right ; they then conclude sadly that their own difficulties in interpretation and mistakes must be due to some fault in themselves. They do not realise that such charts chosen for publication or discussion are always spoken about retrospectively and that it is very easy to be wise after the event.

Furthermore, maps of people in whose life definite *events* have occurred are usually chosen because to the writer or lecturer, it seems necessary to show how well astrological significators can correlate with such events.

A consultant's life would be much simpler if clients always came to talk about such clear-cut happenings, but the fact is that they rarely do. They come because they are unhappy, or puzzled or lonely or worried or unable to decide whether they are on the right or wrong track in handling their lives.

Often they do not wish to tell their feelings to their own families or friends. Also they know that even with the best intent, advice from these will be biased by personal relationship. An astrologer to whom they are unknown will be impersonal and unbiased in reply.

The vicar, who is the subject of this analysis, was unknown to the writer and lived so far away that he could not come for an interview. He has given full permission for both analysis and letters to be published. He wrote because he knew that the consultant was interested in astrology from the psychological point of view. On receiving a request for something in the way of case history, he wrote letters from which the following are shortened extracts.

BIRTH CHART

PROGRESSED DATA   EQUAL HOUSE SYSTEM

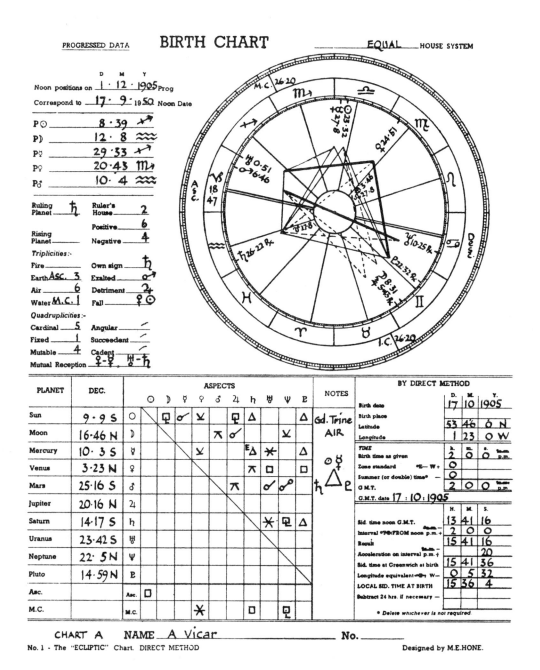

Noon positions on   1 · 12 · 1905 Prog

Correspond to   17 · 9 · 1950 Noon Date

P☉   8 · 39   ♐

P☽   12 · 8   ♒

P☿   29 · 33   ♐

P♀   20 · 43   ♏

P♂   10 · 4   ♒

Ruling Planet ♄	Ruler's House	2	
	Positive	6	
Rising Planet	Negative	4	

Triplicities:-

Fire	Own sign	♄	
Earth ASC. 3	Exalted	♂	
Air 6	Detriment	♃	
Water M.C. 1	Fall	♀☉	

Quadruplicities:-

Cardinal 5	Angular	
Fixed 1	Succeedent	
Mutable 4	Cadent	
Mutual Reception ♀-☿	♅-♄	

PLANET	DEC.		ASPECTS										NOTES		BY DIRECT METHOD			
			☉	☽	☿	♀	♂	♃	♄	♅	♆	♇				D.	M.	Y.
Sun	9 · 9 S	☉		⬓	☌	⊼		⬓	△			△	Gd. Trine AIR	Birth date	17	10	1905
Moon	16 · 46 N	☽					⊼	☌			⛎			Birth place			
Mercury	10 · 3 S	☿				⊼		E△	✶		△			Latitude	53	46	0 N
Venus	3 · 23 N	♀						⊼	□		□		☌♀♅♃	Longitude	1	23	0 W
Mars	25 · 16 S	♂					⊼		☌	⚼			♄△♃	TIME Birth time as given	2h	0m	0s p.m.
Jupiter	20 · 16 N	♃												Zone standard *E— W+	0		
Saturn	14 · 17 S	♄							✶	⬓	△			Summer (or double) time* —	0		
Uranus	23 · 42 S	♅												G.M.T.	2	0	0 p.m.
Neptune	22 · 5 N	♆												G.M.T. date 17 · 10 · 1905			
Pluto	14 · 59 N	♇													H.	M.	S.
Asc.		Asc.	□											Sid. time noon G.M.T.	13	41	16
M.C.		M.C.				✶			□		⬓			Interval *TO/FROM noon p.m.+	2	0	0
														Result	15	41	16
														Acceleration on interval p.m.+			20
														Sid. time at Greenwich at birth	15	41	36
														Longitude equivalent *E+ W—	0	5	32
														LOCAL SID. TIME AT BIRTH	15	36	4
														Subtract 24 hrs. if necessary —			

* Delete whichever is not required.

CHART A   NAME A Vicar   No. _____

No. 1 - The "ECLIPTIC" Chart. DIRECT METHOD   Designed by M.E.HONE.

Extracts from letters from Client to Astrologer

(Numbers refer to comments which follow)

1. " My real problem is whether I am following the true path of my individual destiny. I know this sounds very egotistical but it means so much to those near and dear to me and dependent on me . . . My parents wished me to enter the priesthood of the
2. Church of England. I was drawn towards teaching but I fell in with their wishes because of the sacrifices they had made for me . . .
3. I have always found the study of theology intensely interesting and the human side of
4. the work absorbing but have also always been conscious of something lacking in myself for the work when I try to help people. I have found the limits of orthodoxy
5. irksome and have wished to find truth for myself. Owing to an insatiable curiosity to get to the bottom of things, I have read widely. Now it has sometimes seemed to my more literal-minded parishioners that I am *unsound*.
   I have been drawn towards philosophy and psychology and feel impelled to keep
6. an open mind to all new movements of thought which throw new light on the ancient faith.
7. I try to live by the inner mystic side of Christianity which seems either strange or to mean little to those I serve.
8. This is *a great difficulty* as I am troubled by a barrier, probably an unconscious conflict which saps my energy and robs me of confidence. In a sense I feel I have not
9. found an outlet for a fully creative life. *If only I could know my capacities*, latent or otherwise, to which I ought to give full development, and could use them with confidence for my true path in life, then all other problems would work themselves out.
10. My marriage and home life are happy.
11. *For me, my problem is one of integration and synthesis.*"*

First short general impression of a practised astrologer in relation to the problem

Note carefully that it is in relation *to the problem*, not in regard *to the character* at first.
The interpretation is from the chart by Equal House system. (Numbers refer to extracts above.)

1. Capricorn strength in a chart implies aspiration but with security-seeking.
2. Capricorn strength implies sense of duty.
3. Mercury well placed and well aspected and in Libra implies good brain and interest in others.
4. Capricorn ascendant unassuming.
5. Ruler in Aquarius well-aspected ; M.C. in the investigatory sign, Scorpio.
6. Ruler in Aquarius ; the desire to change the old for the new.
7. Ruler of M.C. and dispositor of Asc.-ruler in conjunction in 12th. (The writer feels strongly that the 12th house has to do with all that is hidden and mystic, including that which is hidden in the unconscious of a person and is thus his urgent driving force. (See article in *Astrology*, September and December 1949.)
8. Neptune's action is subversive when not well aspected. It is in the 6th house (work) opposing Mars, energy, in 12th. Note the way in which the client " speaks his map."
9. Again Capricorn ascendant unassuming. Planets in 5th house (creativity) receive some stressful aspects.

   * Italics by author.

BIRTH CHART

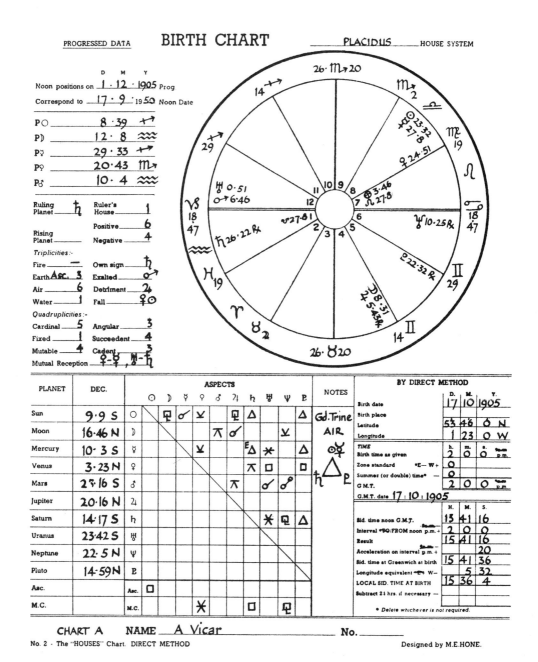

PROGRESSED DATA   PLACIDUS _____ HOUSE SYSTEM

           D   M   Y

Noon positions on 1 · 12 · 1905 Prog

Correspond to 17 · 9 · 1950 Noon Date

P☉	8 · 39	♐
P☽	12 · 8	♒
P☿	29 · 33	♐
P♀	20 · 43	♏
P♂	10 · 4	♒

Ruling Planet ♄   Ruler's House 1

Rising Planet   Positive 6

                     Negative 4

Triplicities:-

Fire	—	Own sign	♄
Earth	Asc. 3	Exalted	♂
Air	6	Detriment	♃
Water	1	Fall	♀☉

Quadruplicities:-

Cardinal	5	Angular	3
Fixed	1	Succeedent	4
Mutable	4	Cadent	3

Mutual Reception ♀-☿ , ♏-♄

PLANET	DEC.	ASPECTS									NOTES	BY DIRECT METHOD			
		☉	☽	☿	♀	♂	♃	♄	♅	♆	♇					
Sun	9·9 S	☉		⚼	☌	⚺		⚼	△			△	Gd.Trine	Birth date	17 10 1905
Moon	16·46 N	☽				⚼	☌				⚺		AIR	Birth place	
Mercury	10· 3 S	☿				⚺		⚼△	✱			△	☿♅	Latitude	53 46 0 N
Venus	3·23 N	♀						⚼	□			□		Longitude	1 23 0 W
Mars	25·16 S	♂					⚼		☌	☍			♄♇	TIME Birth time as given	2 0 0 p.m.
Jupiter	20·16 N	♃												Zone standard •E— W+	0
Saturn	14·17 S	♄							✱	⚼	△			Summer (or double) time• —	0
Uranus	23·42 S	♅												G.M.T.	2 0 0 p.m.
Neptune	22·5 N	♆												G.M.T. date 17 : 10 : 1905	
Pluto	14·59 N	♇												Sid. time noon G.M.T.	13 41 16
Asc.		Asc.	□											Interval •TO/FROM noon p.m. +	2 0 0
M.C.		M.C.		✱		□		⚼						Result	15 41 16

Acceleration on interval p.m. +   20

Sid. time at Greenwich at birth   15 41 36

Longitude equivalent •E W—   5 32

LOCAL SID. TIME AT BIRTH   15 36 4

Subtract 24 hrs. if necessary —

• Delete whichever is not required.

CHART A   NAME A Vicar   No. _____

No. 2 - The "HOUSES" Chart. DIRECT METHOD   Designed by M.E.HONE.

10. Moon, significator of women in a man's life and ruler of 7th, conjunction Jupiter.
11. Conflict in the nature between innate way of self-expression through cusp 10 E.H. (Libran, with Venus not well aspected) and way of self-expression as necessary in the world as it affects him through M.C. (Scorpio with the fighting power of Mars agitated by Uranus and confused by Neptune and working in strong compulsive way through the unconscious.) This point of interpretation is the subject of Chapter 13.

Alternatives

Other astrologers would see this in different ways just as doctors see from different points of view if in consultation together. Also, those using other house systems would interpret accordingly. Throughout the book, maps with Placidean intermediate cusps are given as well as those by Equal House system from which the interpretations are made. These are included since the system is the most commonly used, not because it is intrinsically better than any other but because, until this year (1953), Tables for charting by it were the only ones readily available.

The chart-forms used are produced as now shown at the beginning of this chapter but will be combined in later chapters to save space. Heavy lines denote difficult aspects, lighter lines denoting easier ones ; dotted lines are used for minor difficult aspects.

Astrologers can now compare house-cusps by all systems by reference to the comparative Tables in *The New Waites Compendium of Natal Astrology* *

For this first example, a page of charts by the two systems used in this book and also by those of Campanus, Porphyry and Regiomontanus, is shown. The varying house sizes can clearly be seen. (p. 28).

Note on Natural Graduation System.

Mention should be made of this system, constructed by Colin Evans. No example map has been shown by it since illustrations have been given by old traditional systems only. This new method is dealt with in the book referred to above in which Tables for its use are included with those of others mentioned. Intermediate cuspal degrees for the example are :

XI : 15° 6′ ♐. XII : 29° 11′ ♐. II : 24° 47′ ♒. III : 20° 20′ ♈ (♓ intercepted).

---

* *The New Waites Compendium of Natal Astrology*, by Colin Evans, Routledge, 1953.
† Readers unfamiliar with THE KEYWORD SYSTEM OF INTERPRETATION are referred to Chapter 5.

APPLIED ASTROLOGY

TEN YEAR SHEET*

1950

☉ ☍ ☽
♂ ⚼ ♆ p   ☽ ♒
☽ □ ☉ (O-D)

1951

☉ ⚼ ♆ p
☿ ⚼ ♃ p   ☽ ♒
Asc. ☍ ☉

T ♅ ☌ ♆ ☍ ♂	Spring–summer
T ♄ □ ♅	Spring–autumn
△ ♃ ☽ □ ♂	Autumn
T ♃ □ ♃ ☽ ☍ ♀	Spring
△ ♆ □ ♂ ♅ ♆	Summer

1952

☉ P ♆ r and p
☿ ☌ ♅   ☽ ♓
(1952–53)

T ♆ △ ♇	Autumn
T ♅ ☌ ♆	Spring
T ♄ □ ♆ △ ☽	Summer–autumn
□ Asc. ☌ ☉	Autumn–winter
T ♃ □ ♂ Asc.	Spring
☍ ☉ ☿	Spring
△ ♂ ♅ Asc. ♀	Autumn

1953

♀ ⚹ ♀
□ ♆ p   ☽ ♓
Asc. enters ♉

T ♆ ☌ ☉ △ ♇	Spring–autumn
T ♅ ☍ Asc.	Summer
T ♄ ☌ ☉	Summer
☌ ☿ △ ♄	Spring–autumn
T ♃ △ ♀ ☍ M.C. □ ♄	Spring
☌ ♃ ☽	Summer
△ ☉ ☿ ♄ ☌ ♇	Autumn

1954

♀ ☌ M.C.
□ ♄   ☽ ♓– ♈
P ♂ p

T ♆ ☌ ☉ ☿ △ ♄	Summer–winter
T ♅ □ ☉ □ ☿	Autumn
T ♄ △ ♆	Autumn
T ♃ ☌ ♇ △ ♄ ☉ ☿	Spring
△ M.C. □ ☉ ☿	Autumn

1955

♀ □ ♄ p   ☽ ♈

T ♆ ☌ ☿ △ ♄	Spring–autumn
T ♅ □ ☿ △ M.C.	Summer
T ♄ □ ♄ ☌ M.C.	Winter
T ♃ □ ☉ ☿ △ **M.C.**	Spring
☍ ♄ □ M.C.	Autumn

1956

☉ ✳ ♂ p   ☽ ♈- ♉   T ♆ ☌ ☿   Summer
                                 T ♅ □ ☿   Spring
                                 T ♄ ☍ ♃ D   Winter
                                 T ♃ ☍ ♄   Summer
                                   □ ♃ ☽ ☌ ♀   Summer–autumn
                                   △ ♂ ♅ △ ♇   Autumn

1957

♀ ☍ ♃ p   ☽ ♉   T ♄ ☍ ☽   Summer–autumn
  P ♃ p   T ♃ □ ♅   Spring–autumn
♂ L ☿ p   ☌ ♀   Summer
☿ ☌ ♅   △ ♃ ☽ □♅ ♂   Autumn
                                   ☌ ☉ ☿ □ ♆   Autumn–winter

1958

☿ P ♅ p   ☽ ♉   T ♄ ☍ ♇   Spring–autumn
                                   □ ♀   Summer
                                 T ♃ ☌ ☉ ☿ △ ♄   Summer
                                   △ ♆ □ ♄   Autumn

1959

☿ ⊼ ♃ p   ☽II   T ♄ ☌ ♅ ♂   Spring–autumn
                                 T ♃ ☌ M.C.   Spring–autumn
                                   ☍ D ♃   Autumn
                                   □ ♄   Summer

---

* The main progressions and transits for five or ten years (see similar sheet in Chapter 10) are entered on to these sheets so that a survey can be made of general tendencies in the coming years. In this manner, help can often be given to a person in temporary trouble if the possibility of better times ahead can be deduced. For any special year in the future, fuller details of aspects made by the progressed Moon and by planets in transit can be entered on to the lower half of a No. 3 Chart-form. The planet (or Asc. or M.C.) written first in each entry is understood to be that which is progressed, so it is not necessary that it should be followed by the abbreviation " p ".

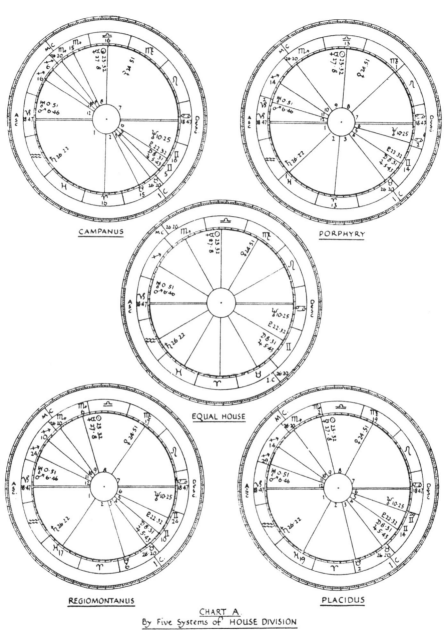

CAMPANUS

PORPHYRY

EQUAL HOUSE

REGIOMONTANUS

PLACIDUS

CHART A.
By Five Systems of HOUSE DIVISION

CHART A

BY FIVE DIFFERENT SYSTEMS OF HOUSE DIVISION

In this example of charting by five different systems of house-division, No. 1, the Ecliptic Chart-form is used in each case, so that the varying sizes of the houses are shown. It should be noticed that the greatest disproportion is by the Campanian system.

Using customary phraseology, it may be said " By these systems, different signs come on different house-cusps, sometimes causing interception of one or more signs, also altering the house-positions of several planets." It can now be realised that the use of both customary chart-forms and customary phraseology is partly responsible for the inattention of many astrologers to the differences caused by the various systems.

Chart-forms such as No. 2, the Houses Chart-form, are almost invariably used when charting by any quadrant system. The house-shapes appear on the paper as if equal. Certain signs and degrees are spoken of as " put on the cusps " and the planets are said to be " put into the houses." Since these varied houses are optional and man-made, it would seem a more factual manner of charting when the start is made with the ecliptic, which is eternal and unalterable, and with the planets entered beside the degrees which designate their zodiacal longitude. After this, having chosen one of the quadrant systems, the phrase used could be brought nearer to accuracy by amending as follows : " By these systems, some house boundaries fall in different signs, sometimes being so close that two or more boundaries fall in one sign, sometimes so far apart that they are separated by the width of one, two or even more signs. This great variation has the effect of enclosing planets within different house-boundaries."

Differences shown in these examples of charting are not at all unusual, nor is the latitude one for which most astrologers are unaccustomed to chart. The birth-place is almost on the same latitude as Liverpool, as is that of Chart E which should be compared.

In this example, by the Regiomontanian and Placidean systems, house-boundaries are far enough apart to include the whole of Libra, Leo and their opposites ; by the Campanian, those signs so included are Virgo, Leo and their opposites, while by the system of Porphyry only Leo and its opposite are not touched by boundaries. It is obvious that the ecliptic remains forever unchanging and unaffected so that interpretation resting on any one sign or another being " intercepted " is on a unsure foundation.

In charting by the Equal House system, the twelvefold equal division of the signs is repeated in the houses. Thus, by analogy, their meaning is carried equally into twelve equal spheres of life-activity. These houses, perpendicular to the ecliptic and meeting at the pole of the ecliptic, are equal the world over, so long as there is an ascending degree from which to start : *they always enclose both the planet and the degree by which it is designated*, thus having no concern with the curious effect of house-boundaries which are not perpendicular to the ecliptic, through the use of which the body of a planet may be in one house-space and its degree in another.

Those interested in comparing these systems should note the variation of the duration of the times of transits of the important planets through these houses of assorted sizes.

A consideration of charting in temperate latitudes by the use of the two chart-forms as shown throughout this book, leads to the conclusion that *in choosing a system of house division for use, the primary decision to be made is not between the rival merits of one system or another but must be in relation to which of two beginnings is to be thought of as basic.* If the invariable ecliptic is to be the base, then no other system but the Equal House system can be decided upon. If the quadrants are to be the base, then the degree culminating at the meridian must always be that of the boundary between ninth and tenth houses and their opposites (M.C. and I.C.) ,no matter what disproportionate sections of the ecliptic are thus enclosed between it and the boundaries cutting the horizon on each side of them (Asc. and Desc.).

In frigid latitudes, many other considerations arise which are not the province of this book, while in tropical latitudes, all systems approximate more to the Equal House system, finally becoming almost the same when the equator is reached.

SKELETON NOTES OF ASTRO-ANALYSIS† FOR CHART OF A VICAR

(The notes are made by the use of the system suggested in *The Modern Text-book of Astrology*. The words *benasp* and *malasp* are used for brevity.)

Category	Significator	Deductions
	General shaping	
Char.	Grand Trine in Air plus Sun	Intelligent, rational, communicative, easy flow of
Ment.	and Moon Air	thought. Gets help from others.
	Cardinal—Air. Positive	Restless, outgoing, forceful.
	Venus, Sun-ruler, point of wide T-sq. (using mid-point of Neptune and Pluto)	Compulsive, awkward in working, as Pluto seeks to throw out, to renew, and Venus, Sun ruler, is squared by them in Virgo from 6th. Difficulties in relationships from work and in unconscious urges.
	Ascendant	
	Capricorn	Practical, cautious, plodding, just, orderly, ambi-
Char.	Saturn benasp	tious. Can wait for ends. Public life, business
Ment.		ability, responsible, industrious. Mentally clever, shrewd. Good in executive position.
Health		Knees, skin, rheumatism.
	Asc-ruler Saturn in Aquarius in 2nd benasp.	Keywords :—Principle of *limitation* and consequent *ambition* working *detachedly* and *for personal gain.* i.e., A cautious conservatism and method will seek to express itself in an intelligent way. He will concentrate on adding to his feeling of owner-ship through this and also make money this way.
	Sun trine Pluto	Easy bringing out of ideas and of getting rid of the unwanted.
Health		Good elimination.
	Sun-ruler Venus, in Virgo in 9th malasp	Keywords :—Urge to *harmony* uneasily expressed immersed in too much *detail* especially when in the sphere of *profound thought.*
	Venus sq. Uranus 9th to 12th	i.e., Relationships awkward ; *wants* harmony but goes about it in too independent a manner. Odd relationships or odd ways of seeking them behind the scenes. Will develop into a neurosis unless *some* outlet given. This should be through happy emotional life and satisfying mental contacts but Jupiter poorly aspected in 5th, not much opportunity.
	Venus sq. Pluto	Again difficulty in harmonising. Too readily throwing-off.

Char.	**Moon** In Gemini, in 5th mainly malasp	Keywords :—*Response* and *manner alert* and *versatile*. Inclination towards *pleasures, risks, love*, but not over-successfully.
Ment. Career	Moon conjunct Jupiter both quincunx Mars 5th to 12th	Energy and initiative in behind-the-scenes ways reflected in an over-quick response to stimulus, an over-creative desire to teach, talk, argue. Exaggeration of forceful manner. Had to do teaching or expounding.
Char. Career	Saturn trine Sun 2nd to 10th	Self expression has to conform to circumstance. Moral well ordered life. Desire to control and order. Progress by work and acceptance of responsibility. Good for business.
Ment.	Saturn trine Mercury 2nd to 10th	Depth of thought. Insistence on detail often annoying to others.
	Saturn trine Pluto	Will throw off difficulties slowly but will do so eventually.
	Saturn sextile Uranus 2nd to 12th	A reformer in secret.
Char.	**Sun** In Libra in 10th (Venus malasp)	Keywords :—*Power and vitality* expressed with desire for *harmony* in *public standing*. i.e., Softening to the harshness of Capricorn, but lack of helpful aspects to Venus means no ease of expression of this. Upset if people don't agree. Therefore balance likely to become a constant comparing of ideas and people. Can be carping. Love of beauty and harmony but unsatisfied.
	Sun p. now in Sagittarius	Vacillating. Eager, mentally questing.
Health		Kidneys, headaches. Fretful if surroundings not harmonious.
Char.	Sun in 10th benasp	Self-expression good, giving power to unite others and to be personally tactful in public life. Diplomatic. Can be very charming.
Ment.	Sun conjunct Mercury	Mind and self in good agreement.
	Sun sesqui : Moon	Again, uneasy expression, conflict.
Ment.	**Mercury** in Libra in 10th benasp	Keywords :—Urge to *communicate* and type of thought are *balanced* and *reasoning*. Wishes to *unite* people by the spoken word and will enhance his public standing in this way.
Career		
Ment.	Mercury trine Pluto	Able to reject and get rid of unwanted ideas.

Char.	**Mars** in Capricorn in 12th	Keywords :—Very *prudent* and careful in the expression of his *energy.* *Conceals* his wants, then expresses them over-emphatically.
	Mars quincunx Jupiter	
	Mars conjunct Uranus in 12th	Powerful, tense ; wilfulness, pent up in Capricorn and hidden in 12th ; a dangerous contact unless expressed in 12th house ways (emotion—psychism —art). Jupiter rules 12th ; a tendency to overdo. A subconscious strife and urge to force the pace, badly out of tune with the Capricorn side but held in check by it.
	Mars opp. Neptune 12th to 6th	Strongly imaginative. Sense of failure because of dreams must encourage his *best* side, i.e., the Capricornian.
	Jupiter in Gemini in 5th Lacks aspects	Keywords :—Desire for *opportunity* and *expansion* in a *versatile* way, in *pleasures* and to do with *children.* Too little outflow for big desires, for happiness and expression of life. Can only be through talk and writing and children.
Char.	**Uranus** in Capricorn, in 12th Uranus opp. mid-point of Neptune and Pluto	Keywords :—*Independent changefulness* has to be held in *check* and kept down in *the unconscious* (12th). This is overdone so that the " self-un- doing " which is consequent causes difficulties and stress with others.
	Uranus sq. Venus	This must be brought to light and faced and used. How ? Force—energy—leadership in independent practicality and organisation ? Can he start a study group and use his energy to instigate research in his interests instead of antagonising others ?
	(Saturn in 2nd)	Although benasp, he feels a lack of money and of love.
Health	Uranus opp. mid-point of Neptune and Pluto in 6th	Nervous stress.
Ment.	Pisces on 3rd Neptune not benasp	Mind too vague and mental concepts tend to be formless. Saturn is good corrective.
	E.H. 10th Libra M.C. Scorpio	Full of innate desire to make his way through diplomatic unifying ways, but in adult life drawn towards the deeper and more mystical side of life and finding difficulty with it.
	Mars not benasp	
	Part of Fortune 8th and N. Node	Real desires towards all true expression of life itself, hence needing fulfilment for his deepest emotions and turning his mind to the hidden and the occult and to life after death.

ASTRO-ANALYSIS*

for A VICAR

by

MARGARET E. HONE

---

* This is the type of cover-page used by the writer for all analyses. In order to save space, it will not be repeated in later chapters.

PROLOGUE*

Owing to the prevalence of certain misunderstandings, it has been thought well to include the following statement before all work.

ASTROLOGY does not constitute an art by which the future can be foretold in detail. This would be fortune-telling and is not possible.

The modern attitude (as I see it) to this age-old knowledge is more or less as follows.

The Universe is *one* and all parts of it work in unison, but our unaided senses are too inadequate to perceive this. It is possible that by measuring parts which are observable, i.e., the planetary movements, we can deduce this working in the lives of human beings. The deductions from the birth map are according to the experience of astrologers through the ages, and especially those working on modern psychological lines.

Any remark on the possibilities for the future should be preceded by the phrase " the likelihood is that " and should be understood to be the probable outcome of the development of the potentialities of that first moment ; and as conditions of life, not as precise events. As it is impossible to continue to reiterate the phrase, it should be understood.

Dates given are approximate, but are calculated as exactly as possible for the chart under consideration. Though they may point to events, their main use is intended as a guide to what type of helpful activity, or non-activity, is to be stressed at the time.

ASTROLOGY attempts to indicate a life-pattern, but there are more ways than one in which these may be worked out.

NOTE ON CHART†

The signs of the Zodiac are of varying importance in different natal charts. " Popular " astrology has emphasised the one containing the Sun, since everyone can ascertain it by knowing the date of birth.

Serious astrologers are aware that the sign ascending over the horizon at birth is of equal, or even greater importance. The degree rising in this sign can only be computed when the *moment* of birth is known, and is therefore individual to the person for whom the chart is made.

Your chart shows that :—

The sign ascending is Capricorn.

The sign containing the Sun is Libra.

You would therefore be described astrologically as :—

" Capricornian, with Sun in Libra."

Hence, subject to the many subtle modifications imposed by the angular relationships of the planets at your birth moment, and the emphasis on the other signs, you are very largely a compound of the characteristics known to be observable in those for whom the above signs are important.

Except to those to whom it is familiar, technical astrological terminology will not be used in the following analysis. The main astrological correlatives of every deduction made from the chart will be entered in the margin of the copy filed for future reference, and can be obtained by arrangement, if required.

* This statement precedes *every* interpretation sent out by the writer. In order to save space, it will not be repeated in later chapters.

† This note precedes all analyses done by the writer. In order to save space it will not be repeated in later chapters.

ANALYSIS OF CHARACTER AND DISCUSSION OF PROBLEMS

Significators*

♂ ☌ ♅ in 12th
⊼ ♃ in 5th

Your chart is of the greatest interest because it portrays a man of complex CHARACTER in which the outstanding point is that strength and energy are subdued and held back and thus find insufficient channels for expression, causing irritation and nervous strain.

Asc. ♑

Essentially, you are practical, cautious, just, orderly and can work in a plodding way and wait for your results. You are industrious and have an excellent sense of responsibility and a strong ambition to succeed in your aims.

♄ in ♒

♄ in 2nd

In these aims, you wish to bring your organising, planning abilities to a practical ordering of more abstract conceptions and through this you hope to satisfy an urge towards stability of mind and to make up for a feeling of inadequacy in more material possessions. Though you express yourself as being happy in your home life, you have a sense of insufficient satisfaction in your feeling of love and possessiveness, and one of your ways of compensating for this is through a concentration on mental pursuits and the happiness thus found through the possession of stability through knowledge.

☿ in 10th
△ ♄

☉ in ♎ in 10th

☽ ☌ ♃ in 5th

From one point of interpretation after another, the same impression comes—the picture of a man who has strong desires for expression through affection, through a feeling of unison in life, through love of beauty and ease and colourful harmony, but who has had to conform to circumstance and realise that the very effort to produce unison often causes rifts.

♀ malasp

☽ ☌ ♃ in II
☉ ≏ benasp
Asc. ♑ but
♅ ☌ ♂ in 12th
☍ ♆ (ruler of
natural 12th)
♃ in detriment
and malasp
♂ ☍ ♆
⊼ ♃

Outwardly, you have a genial charm which is very attractive. You are a good talker and a pleasant companion, but you have a sense of failure in results, the roots of which lie deep and are not easy to explain. Firstly, there is lack of *opportunity* for creative expansion. Then, there is a highly vivid imagination so that you dream of that to which you cannot attain. But beneath all this and more deeply in your unconscious self, is a powerful drive to independent self-expression. There is a tendency to overdo that which is desired, an urge to force the pace and be the leader of thought amongst those surrounding you. All this has to *conform* to orthodoxy, as you yourself said, but also to a strong sense of prudence and caution in *yourself*.

♂ ♅ ☍ ♆ but
♄, ruler, malasp

♀ □ ♇ in Ⅱ

The versatile, questing, initiatory, disruptive and rebellious side of yourself is for ever at strife with the more solid and quietly ambitious side. There must be times when this comes to the surface and breaks out and then your difficulties begin, as you are apt to spoil relationships with others by an overquick expression of urgent ideas. The possible way of resolving this difficulty will be discussed later.

* Since the pages of " Notes " can be sent to a typist to be returned for filing if desired, longhand is used for significators. In the analysis, the symbols are added by the astrologer, in his carbon copy only, so that typing for client can be full page.

☿ ♎ in 10th

Grand △
♓ 3rd
M.C. ♏
♆ malasp

♆ 6th

MENTALLY, you are intelligent and rational and with an easy flow of thought with which you seek to unite people by your ideas. You cannot help but use this ability to enhance your public standing and to draw to you many who will uphold you and help you on your way. However, there is another ingredient in your mental make-up, already alluded to as strong imagination. This is a turning to the intangible and what you rightly called the mystical. Though much in sympathy with such leanings, your chart does show that, in your work, especially in your desire to give service to others, you set up a tenseness and strain in yourself which can be your own undoing if you allow it to wander or become diffuse and too unreal.

There is much else to say about you, but this seems to be the moment to sum up the roots of your dissatisfaction and the way to better integration.

Jung says that the most important problems of life are all *fundamentally* insoluble. They can never be solved, but only *outgrown*. He says that people do this by *accepting* the problem and by *developing further by means of it*. He says that a new thing grows, sometimes from within, sometimes from without, and that this seems to flow out of the *stream of time*. This " stream of time " is what the astrologer is trying to assess in the life, by the interpretation of the changing factors as he understands them.

♄, ruler, benasp

Therefore, the operative word seems to be *acceptance* and the corollary to that seems to be patience. To accept a thing, one must know it. Once accepted and brought into the open, it can be dealt with. " The art of letting things happen " can be learnt, complexes will not turn into conflicts, and wholeness will be achieved through self knowledge and integration.

☽ ☌ ♃ ♊
☉ ♎

♂ ☌ ♅ malasp
⚹ ♃ in 5th

Asc. ♑
♄, ruler, benasp

In your case, the easy versatility in one side of you and the ready charm of manner which is so natural to you, both obscure the rebellious forcefulness which presses you to sudden action, to the search for newness at any price, and the almost autocratic desire for self expression and creativity.

This is the most *compulsive* side of you, but it is *not the best side*. The best side is the cautious, orderly, solid, serious, responsible side. It is a pity that you have no astrological knowledge, for you could see this for yourself in the shaping of your chart so easily. *Always* you are on the right track and moreover will improve both your work and your prestige when you stress the less rebellious but more prudent side, when you deliberately " lay on " the charm of manner and hold back a certain carping tendency which stems from a perpetual desire to balance people up, to contrast their attractive and unattractive ways, to vacillate, to hesitate to be whole-hearted about them, because you can so well see the less good traits in them as well as the good.

6th and 10th

☉ ♎

♀ malasp

♂ ♅ in 12th
malasp. ♑.

What is to be done with the enormous force in your unconscious that urges you to be disruptive and upset the calm, cool exterior ?

♀ □ ⛢ □ ♇

♂ ☍ ♆
♄ △ ☿ in 10th

Asc. ♑
☽ ☌ ♃ in 5th
Use M.C. in ♏
♂ 12th

⛢ ⚹ ruler, ♄

Use ♄
and ☽ ☌ ♃

Asc. ♑
☉ ♎
⛢ in 12th

♄ benasp

☽, ♃ ♊
☿ benasp
Ruler benasp

♄ △ ☿

Sun-ruler in ♍

♄ in 2nd benasp

Asc. ♑

☽ ♊

Firstly, recognise its existence. Secondly sit back and interestedly *watch* it at work. Watch it trying to push you into high-handed behaviour which antagonises people. Watch it trying to force you into sudden unguarded expression of what you *feel intuitively* rather than what you think rationally. Next, with the excellent strategy-forming side of you, think out ways in which this pent-up energy can be expressed and externalised.

What can you do which is practical and constructive and creative ?

On the sheerly practical side, can you grow things in your garden and make it productive both of food and of beauty ? Can you use the submerged energy in orderly writings rather than arguing ? Can you put your imaginings and dreams on paper as paintings ? And finally, and most importantly, could you collect together those people who fail to understand your creative purpose in renewing the old truths of religion with vivid life and whose materialism has obscured the mysticism behind the symbols which have become ordinary to them, and could you form a study group in which you would lead their thought and educate their minds in the withdrawn surroundings of the study rather than electrify them too suddenly by pronouncements in public ?

In this way, you will solve your own conflict and break down the barrier which you felt was rendering you impotent and find more outlet for creativity.

Above all, do not aim *too* high. Your true path in life is through patient consolidation and the use of your very courteous geniality, fully accepting the deeper urge to rebelliousness which could lead you to a more brilliant dynamism and giving this every opportunity for expression, but *always* with control.

To speak shortly of other matters, your CAREER is not misplaced. Indeed you could have been a teacher as you have the mentality for it and an interest in children ; however, in the more hidden side of religious life, you should find a deeper satisfaction than would have come to you from academic life.

You have a depth of thought and an ability and a grasp of the details of an argument which would have been a little too much for children and are better in expounding your ideas to adults.

Had you adopted a teaching career, you would have made a success in scientific studies and thus in the training of older students.

You should be successful at making money in your career, but your present work gives you no opening for this.

In business and finance you could have done well for you would have used the careful, watchful, far-seeing side of your character. Could you build up a subsidiary money-making activity by writing, thus using the submerged creativity, the strong imagination and the desire to feel better off ?

☉ ♎
♇ □ ♀,
♀ malasp
⊕ 8th
♀ malasp
6 planets in Air

In your FRIENDSHIPS, FAMILY CONTACTS and in fact all RELATIONSHIPS, you easily free yourself from unwanted intimacies, but find it difficult to make new ones. You are apt to be too captious about people, not wishing to accept them with all their faults. You need affection and deep satisfaction and can become moody and tense if you feel lack of harmony in your life. Your chart does show something of a lack of full opportunity in this way, so it may be as well to recognise this as part of your pattern and to make up for lack of emotional satisfaction by fullness of mental interests.

☿, ruler 6th benasp
♀ ruler ♎ malasp
Asc. ♑

HEALTH should be good on the whole, though headaches may be caused by faulty kidney action. In every way, try to avoid those things which are said to be contributary causes to rheumatism.

♋ 7th
☽ ☌ ♃ ⚻ ♂ 12th
☽ ☌ ♃ in 5th in ♊
but other aspects
⚼ and ⚻

Your WIFE should be of the greatest help to you, being of the type to bring you out and help you in every way, but she will not always sympathise with the rebel side of you. Your CHILDREN should be charming, lively, expansive and versatile, bringing you happiness but occasioning you some stress and irritation at times.

☉ ♎, Asc. ♑
Both rulers benasp
grand △

There is so much in your life to be thankful for, ease of speech, grace of expression, ability to order and control and, above all, an ability to take advantage of help from others in the advancement of your career, that, on balance, you must feel that those understandable drives to discontent are not so very upsetting after all, but can be used to creative achievement in a new line to be thought about and planned.

Note to Students on interpretation of Present Conditions and Future Possibilities.

In regard to all sections such as that which now follows, if a client does not know what to expect from astrological assessment, explain to him that you can do no more than *examine trends*. If he thinks that an astrologer should tell him *exactly* what lies in the future for him explain that you are *not* a fortune-teller and that he has a wrong idea of astrology. Always preface work with a Prologue in which comment is made about your own attitude to the use of astrological technique.

PRESENT TIME 1950–51

☉ p ☍ ☽ r

It is not surprising that you should ask for some clarification of your life this year, for you have come to a time which is often alluded to as a " Full Moon " in life, in other words, a time of fruition, of ripening. You have been growing to maturity in understanding and now is your time to drop the seeds of knowledge which have become ready to be the beginnings of fuller growth in others.

♐ ☍ ♊

The parts of your chart which are cut across by this are those to do with talking, lecturing and writing and you should definitely have some result from these now.

☉ p ☍ ♃r
in 5th

Three years ago, you must have felt a definite urge to expand in this direction and have been irritated at any setbacks, but now is the better time.

☉ entered ♐

Are you sensitive to a change which has taken place in you since *eight years ago* ? At that time began an alteration which was working in your unconscious and should be well established by now. By the tone of your letter, it seems to be so. It should have begun with a restlessness both of body and of mind so that you wanted to be out and about more and get more exercise and yet you wanted to spend time in your study, going more and more deeply into more mystical and occult studies and also into more philosophical reading.

♂ ⚻ ♆ r and p in 6th

Desires will never be wholly fulfilled with you and there has been a strain connected with this which has been partly to do with health. You have been exerting a great deal of energy and finding it foiled and baffled. The feeling must have been comparable to hitting hard and finding your punch unresisted by a feather pillow. The condition does not disperse until *autumn* 1951. It will irritate you less if you simply realise it as part of your present pattern. Also, it would be well to see that you have no toxic disturbance due to faulty digestive troubles. This could be a contributory cause to the psychological feeling of defeatism.

☊ in 6th
♆ in (natal) malasp

☽ 2nd

This year, your mind should turn to money making and the inclusion of scientific interests or those to do with radio, television, or photography.

♀ p ⚻ ♇ p
T ♆ □ Asc.
T ♅ ☌ ♆ in 6th

There is a slight stress shown in your dealings with others. Your tendency is towards too much impatience. Your natural tendency is otherwise and it again seems that there is a faulty health condition behind this. Could you have a medical check ?

DETAILS OF 1950–51

November

T ♆ □ Asc. repeats during year

There is a disturbing lack of clarity which affects you and, again, it may be that a physical toxic condition should be dealt with and removed. You are likely to be dreamy and introspective and hence to make mistakes carelessly because of your pre-occupation.

7th–15th

T ♂ ☌ ♅ ♂ in 12th

Though these dates are past, they should be mentioned as they should have marked an intensification of your inner life. On the outer and practical side, there may have been repercussions of over hasty speech and action causing some irritation at home.

30th

T ♂ ☌ Asc.

You should be careful around this day lest you betray yourself into sudden, unthinking behaviour which you would regret later.

December

1st

T ♄ □ ♅ repeats during year

For some days around this date, you are likely to feel a heaviness and a limitation of inspirational thought. Rest and quiet will put this right.

1951

⊙ p ⊼ ♆ p
☿ p ⊼ ♃ p
Asc. p ☍ ⊙
☽ p ☌ ♄

On the whole, this is not an easy year. You have not yet found the line which you should follow though you are working towards it. *1953* will begin a new phase.

You will be trying to do too much and may overtire yourself, which will not help in your dealings with others or in your profession.

January
6th–19th

T ♂ ☌ ♄ in 2nd

T ♃ □ ♃ □ ☽ in 5th

T ♅ ☍ ♂

You should be making very great efforts to achieve some end, involving money, but with much difficulty. If you could wait a month, the difficulties will be less. There is a direct stirring up of your most restless and inflammatory side and it appears to connect with matters to do with children and also with creative ability in mental ways.

The week centring round the 14th is explosive and calls for care.

February

T ♄ □ ♅

Towards the end of the month there is a damping of the more restless side of you and possible annoying inability to make a desired change.

March
16th–30th

T ♆ □ Asc.
T ♃ □ ♇ ☍ ♀

This is the most difficult part of the month, affecting you personally and your health, while the latter part calls for extreme care and tact in your dealings with others.

April
5th

T ♃ △ M.C.

Improvement so far as profession is concerned.

25th

T ♃ □ ♅

Urgent desires find little outlet or else find opportunity of expression which cannot materialise.

May
10th

Difficult aspects to and from ♂
(♂ in 12th)

This repeats the over-stimulation of 14th January. The urgent drive to action stems from your unconscious and is a matter about which you will not be disposed to argue, but you will be wise to try to use the very sane controlling side of you to think twice before speaking your mind.

29th

T ♂ ☌ ♃

So long as care is used and nervous stress avoided, much good could happen to-day. Opportunities could be forced. Action could be taken.

June
2nd

T ♂ ☌ ☽

Activity which affects your wife.

T ♃ □ ♆

15th
Avoid woolliness of thought.

23rd

T ♂ ☌ ♇

Too explosive for comfort, but a good day if you need to set off a fuse which will have the effect of clearing or dispersing what had been in your way.

July

☽ p △ ♇
to △ ☉ Aug.

Against a good background of greater serenity, there are several slightly disturbing days.

14th

T ♅ ☌ ♆ in 6th

Stressful in work with repercussion on health.

19th

T ♂ ☌ ♆

As above, but for other reasons, greater care is needed. The time *could* be used to advantage in connection with non-material things. This is difficult to express except by saying that one can only reach the clouds of inspiration by taking one's feet off the ground, but that there is always danger in such loss of touch with reality.

Loss of contact with reality might indeed be through anaesthetic or other escapism at this time.

August

T ♄ □ ♅

The middle of the month is a time when you would feel on edge and anxious for change.

September

T ♆ □ Asc.
T ♃ □ ♆

A more difficult month.

October

☽ p □ M.C. ☌
♄ p
T ♄ △ ♃ □ ♂
△ ☽

Not an easy month though one in which you could bring success from a financially rewarding piece of work. This seems to be either through the help of your wife or else to be very acceptable to her.

1952

☉ p P ♆ r and p
☽ in ♓

The year has great possibilities of success through intuitive work which has been gradually achieved. Writing or publishing could be successful. In yourself, you will be entering on a two-year period of greater touch with the intangibles and should use this time to develop any aptitude for psychic or artistic work.

1953

☿ p ☌ ♅ r
(1952–53)
Asc. p into ♉
and in 4th

T ♃ 5th
T ♄ ☌ ☉

Changes must come into your life at the turn of the year. It sounds paradoxical to say so, but your *inner* motivation will be towards more stability. You may come into some new possessions for the home or even a new house. The time is beneficial for your own creativity and for your children. Your mind will be more than ever concentrated on what is below the surface and, by now, you will have gained a greater understanding of such things and should be able to bring out what you have pondered on during the last two years. The year will not be without its serious side, but progress should be solid and happy.

1954

T ♃ in 6th
△ planets in 10th
♀ p ☌ M.C. but
□ ♄ in 2nd

Health and opportunity for work should be good. In your profession, there should be advancement through work with others, but you will need to watch the financial side of any new arrangement.

1955

♀ p ☌ M.C. □ ♄
☽ p in ♈ in 4th

While finance still calls for care, personal energy is at its best with good results at home.

1956

T ♃ ☍ ♄ but
☉ p ✶ ♂ p
(♂ r in 12th)

Though you seem to take on extra responsibilities which affect your family life, there are many compensations in this busy year. You should be able to reach your objectives and often through having trained your unconscious self to work with you and for you. You yourself might prefer to put it that you are conscious of and willing to be in tune with unseen guidance.

1957

☿ p ☌ ♅ r
♂ p ∟ ☿ p
♀ p ☍ ♃ p
T ♃ ☌ ♀

You need to be very careful to watch your mental reactions. You will be in a changeable mood when sudden flashes of inspiration can come to you, but, even so, it would be wise to scrutinise them carefully. There will be difficulties at home, but there should be an excellent and happy summer.

1958

☿ p P ♅ p

♃'s transits

Mental receptivity is still swift and should be used for literary output. The summer and autumn should be very much more successful than usual in every way. There should be a professional opportunity which should be taken. Income and health should benefit.

1959

T ♄ ☌ ♅ ♂
T ♃ ☌ M.C.
☍ ☽ ♃ 5th

The spring and autumn both bring times of crisis in that sudden action is called for and you need all your powers of organising. Professional success may conflict with the interests of the children.

Dates should be considered to be approximate. Details of further years can be supplied and should be asked for in the previous autumn in good time.

Extract from letter from Client to Astrologer.

It is hard to satisfy the natural desire of the reader to know how this was received by the client without appearing to be saying " I was right." It must be understood that such confirmations are given exactly as written and solely in the cause of helping the student to find out how true astrological interpretation can be.

The reply (much shortened) was as follows :—

" I find the chart very interesting and so far as one can judge of oneself, the analysis seems very accurate.

" The reference to the change which began eight years ago and the conflict or struggle that took place between wanting to get out and about, and the desire for study, is singularly accurate. Material shortage has dogged my footsteps ; much has had to be done on an income just sufficient, with rigid economy, for family needs. I am not complaining, but stating facts.

" Gardening has been my salvation at times and I can do a bit while minding the children. I do love colour and harmony but, alas, cannot paint.

" Quiet steady work, or as you put it ' *the consolidation of results*' has given me the happiest times of my life . . . yet a tendency to dolce far niente and inertia is there and needs counteracting as well as the rampageous subconscious drive. I am fascinated by the analysis and impressed by the fact that the Universe is such a close-knit unity . . . Astrology seems to offer an objective guidance which is not dependent on whims and moods.

" I am taking the relevant advice quite seriously as I hope it will help me to find the right track . . ."

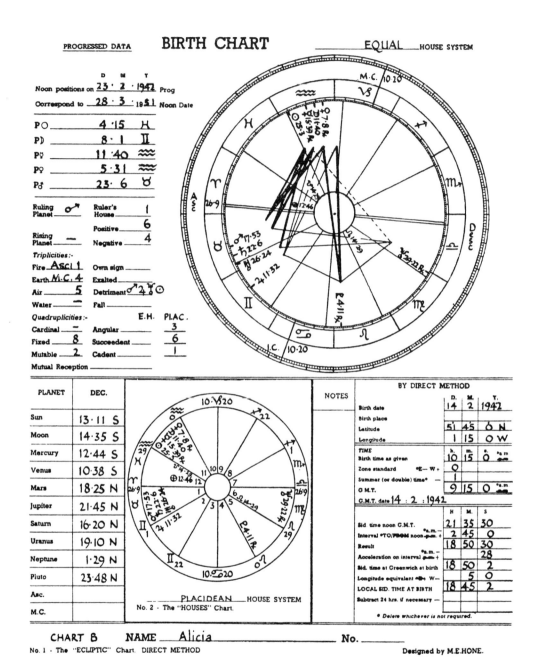

PROGRESSED DATA   **BIRTH CHART**   _____ EQUAL HOUSE SYSTEM

	D	M	Y	
Noon positions on	23 · 2 · 1942			Prog
Correspond to	28 · 3 · 1951			Noon Date

P☉	4·15 ♓
P☽	8·1 ♊
P☿	11·40 ♒
P♀	5·31 ♒
P♂	23·6 ♉

Ruling Planet ♂	Ruler's House ___ 1
	Positive ___ 6
Rising Planet ___ —	Negative ___ 4

Triplicities:-
Fire **Asc** 1   Own sign _____
Earth **M.C.** 4   Exalted _____
Air   5   Detriment ♂ 2 ♃ ☉
Water   —   Fall _____

Quadruplicities:-   E.H.   PLAC.
Cardinal ___ —   Angular ___   3
Fixed ___ 8   Succeedent ___ 6
Mutable ___ 2   Cadent ___   1
Mutual Reception _____

PLANET	DEC.
Sun	13·11 S
Moon	14·35 S
Mercury	12·44 S
Venus	10·38 S
Mars	18·25 N
Jupiter	21·45 N
Saturn	16·20 N
Uranus	19·10 N
Neptune	1·29 N
Pluto	23·48 N
Asc.	
M.C.	

PLACIDEAN HOUSE SYSTEM
No. 2 - The "HOUSES" Chart.

NOTES

BY DIRECT METHOD

	D.	M.	Y.
Birth date	14	2	1942
Birth place			
Latitude	51	45	0 N
Longitude	1	15	0 W

TIME	h.	m.	s.	
Birth time as given	10	15	0	a.m.
Zone standard E— W+	0			
Summer (or double) time*	1			
G.M.T.	9	15	0	a.m.
G.M.T. date 14 : 2 : 1942				

	H.	M.	S.
Sid. time noon G.M.T.	21	35	30
Interval *TO/FROM noon a.m.— p.m. +	2	45	0
Result	18	50	30
Acceleration on interval p.m. +			28
Sid. time at Greenwich at birth	18	50	2
Longitude equivalent E+ W—		5	0
LOCAL SID. TIME AT BIRTH	18	45	2
Subtract 24 hrs. if necessary —			

* Delete whichever is not required.

CHART **B**   NAME ___ Alicia ___   No. _____
No. 1 - The "ECLIPTIC" Chart. DIRECT METHOD   Designed by M.E.HONE.

CHAPTER 7

ASTROLOGICAL HELP TO A PARENT

Chart B.—ALICIA, ON GOING TO SCHOOL

Reason for Inclusion

THIS analysis illustrates one of the ordinary difficulties in life which come to a parent. Alicia was an only child and had been brought up in the somewhat specialised atmosphere of a loving home and a kindergarten school run on a carefully thought-out principle. It was difficult for her mother to make the decision to allow her to go into the bigger world of a boarding school. She felt that perhaps she was in too close contact with her child to be the best judge of the matter and that the opinion of an astrologer might be of use.

The usual notes were made in preparation for an interview. After a query, it was decided that the child should not come too, as it would be easier to talk without her. On hearing the " Notes," the mother expressed her extreme interest in astrological technique, saying that it would have been quite unnecessary to have brought the little girl since everything about her seemed to be known already !

SKELETON NOTES OF ASTRO-ANALYSIS FOR CHART OF ALICIA*

(The notes are made by the use of the system suggested in *The Modern Text-book of Astrology*. The words *benasp* and *malasp* are used for brevity.)

Category Significators		*Deductions*
Char.	**General Indications** 8 planets in fixed signs	Good sound upbringing very essential for this child as she has sterling qualities of reliability and stability but can be just as stable and set in bad ways as in good, therefore early training matters enormously.
	Satellitium in Aquarius ; another in Taurus with M.C. in Capricorn	Strong in her mental ideas and aims with decided views in life and ambition but in a reserved cautious way, going over to stubbornness if she doesn't like what is happening.
Char.	**Ascendant** Asc. in Aries but very much modified by ruler in Taurus in 1st with ruler M.C.	Keywords :—*Lively, assertive, energetic,* but also stable and reliable ; can be stubborn or inert. Loves the good things of the earth, good food and, when older, good wine and entertaining. Good
Money	(Taurus on 2nd)	food sense. Has feeling for building, making, conserving. Can be possessive and jealous of her own things and people and too insistent about them.

* Readers unfamiliar with THE KEYWORD SYSTEM OF INTERPRETATION are referred to Chapter 5.

	Dispositor of one satellitium in mutual reception with dispositor of the other	Not an easy child to bring up as her nature contains such contradictions. It is no use saying she *is* this or she *should be* the other.

Her essential nature is to give surprises to those who have charge of her and to show *different* sides of her very complex character at different times.

Mars

Health — Asc.-ruler Mars in Taurus in 1st, sq. Sun, Moon and Mercury (see detail in paragraphs referring to these)

Keywords :—*Energy* working in *stable*, but *possessive* ways and very *personally*, i.e., she can be too drastic and can bring trouble on herself by her own forcefulness. She is rather like a volcano in her long moods of charming quiescence with sudden outbreaks which can be self-destructive as they will injure her in the eyes of her companions in life.

Con. Saturn (which is also Con. Uranus)

Strong drive to action in an assertive way, held down and then let loose.

Sun

Char. — Sun in Aquarius in 10th malasp

Keywords :—*Power and vitality* working *detachedly* perhaps *scientifically, in her way of expression in the world.*

i.e., She will not have too easy a time finding her niche in life as there is *such a strong element of contradiction* in her make-up that she will be at odds with herself. It is necessary that she should quite happily *realise* that she is strongly pulled two ways and should learn to watch her reactions to circumstances and see herself as an extremely interesting study of which she will never come to the end.

Sq. Mars, Saturn and Uranus, all in Taurus

Her urge towards independent thought and action and towards being " different " and unusual will always be at variance with her desire that things should remain as they are so that she is comfortable and secure.

She can be wayward and awkward, but what impels her will be the desire to be different from whatever is around her.

Career — (Jupiter benasp)

The best way to help her is to give her a very *varied* education, not only in languages but in science. If she has the educational backing to pursue different lines of thought, she will then do this in a *trained* way, not just as a petulant changefulness.

Health — Sq. Saturn in Taurus in 1st

Her health will be under a certain amount of strain too. Circulation and heart must be cared for. Also throat and all inflammatory conditions ; colds and catarrhal conditions. Can have moods of depression and feelings of inadequacy and timidity about life. She can take responsibility and is likely to get it, probably in relation to one of her parents.

Sq. Uranus	In spite of her " stickability," she can go off at a tangent and upset all calculations, suddenly changing her mind in an autocratic way.
Sq. Mars	Can be pugnacious.
Sun-ruler Uranus in Taurus in 2nd dispositor of satellitium Con. Saturn in 1st	Keywords : Tendency to *unpredictability*, *conservatively* held to in all *possessive and personal ways* (paradox). i.e., Can have *violently wayward*, *moody*, reckless moments when she hates authority or control, yet she *likes* order *in her way* ! This child cannot possibly be *ordinary* she must be helped to be *out-of-the-ordinary* in a suitable way ! She can, in fact, be quite *outstanding*.
Venus Venus in Aquarius in 10th (Satellitium also)	Keywords :—Urge to *harmony* working *detachedly* sometimes *rebelliously*, in what will be her " world " when older.
Travel trine Jupiter	i.e., To her, pleasantness in life means sticking to her own ways which won't necessarily be those of other people and developing much more in later girlhood when she can use her excellent mind to broaden her outlook by travel. She should be allowed to learn several languages and go to the
Schools (Mercury also trine Jupiter)	countries where they are spoken. Finishing schools abroad would be good for her.
Char. (but Saturn con ruler in Taurus in 1st)	Every tendency in this chart is balanced by an opposite one ! She can be very genial and expansive but also can shut up like the proverbial clam.
Char. Conjunct Moon (in Aquarius)	Pleasant manner, nice smile, should have good speaking and singing voice which should be trained, if not for singing itself, then for reading, recitation and possible broadcasting in the future.
Opp. Pluto (in 4th)	Will put up with things for a long time with great patience and then explode and get rid of them. This is very tiresome in home-life.
Moon Char. Moon in Aquarius in 10th	Keywords :—*Response* is in a *detached* way and with leanings towards interest in *public affairs* when older.
Con. Mercury and Venus, sq. Mars and trine Jupiter (exact) (with Asc. Aries)	Again many contradictions all of which confirm the unusual brilliant nature of the child. Charming, intelligent, genial, fortunate, but argumentative, over-forceful, dogmatic, requiring good training as already said.

Mercury

Ment.

Mercury in Aquarius in 10th
Sq. Mars, sq. Saturn, but trine
Jupiter

Keywords :—*Communicativeness* in *detached way*
in relation to her *outer life.* More emphasis on the
freedom-loving, cool, going-its-own-way type,
personally and mentally, *but it must never be
forgotten* that *however* she behaves, she has her
other side which craves for a stable background of
solid worth in life. She can be sharp in speech and
gloomy in mind but this must be trained to be
quick repartee and amusing satire rather than
hurtful causticness and to be a seriousness of mind,
not moody petulance. She can be gay and very good
fun and this is her *best* side.

Jupiter

Char.

Jupiter in Gemini in 2nd
benasp

Keywords :—*Expansion* in an *alert, versatile way*
in relation to her *belongings and feelings.*
i.e., With all her difficult ways, she has the *finest
possible corrective* which is a gay, cheerful, pleasant
way of talking and behaving. A happy way of
riding over everything. She will attract opportunities and take them and have a good share of
" luck " in life.

Money

Char.

Saturn

Saturn in Taurus in 1st

Good money sense.

Keywords :—*Limitation* in *possessive, stable* way,
very *personally.*
i.e., She will find that with all her good backing in
life, she will have circumstances which hold her
back and make her think and stop her from doing
all she wants to do, probably from (1) a physical
reason or (2) responsibility put on her.

Career

(ruler M.C.)

Neptune

Health

Neptune in Virgo in 6th trine
Saturn and Uranus

Work

sesqui. Mercury

Keywords :—*Nebulousness* in a detailed *dis-
criminating* way in anything to do with *health and
work.*
i.e., She will be idealistic about what she wants to
do in the way of work, especially if for others and
will have sensible (if fussy) ideas about caring for
her health.

REPORT ON INTERVIEW

Significators*

Satellitium con-
taining ☉, ☽ in ♒.
Another in ♉
containing ♂,
Asc.-ruler.

When you look at Alicia's chart, you will be reminded of the quite
unusual formation which I pointed out to you. For any person to
have a group of planets in one part of the Zodiac is an indication of
special emphasis on the qualities indicated by that part. It is then
obvious that, if there are *two* parts thus heavily stressed, there are *two*
centres of emphasis.

* Entered on astrologer's carbon copy only.

Dispositors of these
formations in
mutual reception

Moreover, in her case, the one interacts with the other to a surprisingly close extent. Thus, in her own way, she will have to go through life showing forth the traits of these two different sides of her nature. She can never thoroughly combine them as they are so dissimilar but she is more likely to swing from the one side to the other, often disconcertingly and unexpectedly. This will make her inexplicable to those who do not really know her, but fascinating to those who have come to realise this dichotomy.

8 planets in fixed
signs

She is stable, reliable, trustworthy, solid and cautious, which qualities could also mean a slowness in some ways, particularly in getting off the mark. This you have instanced in the fact that, at nine, she still does not properly read and write.

☉ ♒
Asc.-ruler in ♉
Asc. ♈

She is not an easy child to bring up because of these contradictions. But it will be much easier to plan for her now that you realise that this truly *is so* ; that she is not " this " or " that " but definitely of two sides, and *both* very strongly marked in her.

♉
♒

With all her sensible, practical side, yet her essential nature is also to give surprises to those who have charge of her and to show her *different* sides at different times.

♀ in ♒

To her, pleasantness in life means sticking to her own ways which will not necessarily be those of other people. She will develop much more in later girlhood when she can use her excellent mind and broaden her outlook by travel. She should be allowed to learn several languages and to visit the countries where they are spoken. Her love of animals and the things of the good earth will always remain with her and she should have a good " food " sense which can be turned to practical use. She will also have a good money sense.

♐ 9th
♃ benasp

strong ♉
♃ in 2nd

♀ △ ♄
but
♄ in ♉

Every tendency in this nature is balanced by an opposite one ! Alicia can be very genial and expansive but also she can shut up like the proverbial clam.

♀ ☌ ☽
Ruler in ♉

She should have a pleasant manner, nice smile and noticeably good speaking voice, which could also be good for singing.

Planets in 10th
☐ those in 1st

She will not have too easy a time in finding her niche in life because the strong element of contradiction in her may make her be at odds with herself so it is splendid that you have chosen this way of finding it out and seeing that she should be enabled to understand herself, quite happily and acceptingly. She can thoroughly enjoy watching herself and her reactions to circumstances and can realise herself as a most interesting study of which she will never come to the end ! She can do this without becoming morbidly introspective as she has such an outreaching mind which will study so many other things besides.

☿ in ♒
☐ ♄ but
△ ♃

Asc. ♈
☉ ♒
Asc.-ruler in
♉ in 1st

Strong ♒

☉ □ ♂
  □ ♄
♄ in 1st

Satellitium ♉
☉ □ ♅

Asc. ruler ♂
Yet ☌ ♄

Full 10th

☽ ♒ ☌ ♀ ☿

♀ in ♒

Strong ♉

☿ □ ♂

♃ in ♊
△ ♀

♃ in 2nd
but ♄ ruler
M.C. in 1st

♌ on 5th
☉ in ♒
□ ♂, ♄ ♅
Asc. ♈

Her urge to independent thought and action, towards being different and unusual will always be at variance with the desire that things should remain as they are, keeping her comfortable and secure. She can be wayward, awkward, difficult and tiresome but she will be impelled by that forceful, assertive urge-to-be-different.

The best way to help her is to *allow* her to be " different," to bring her up with a very varied education, not only in languages but in science. If she has the educated ability to pursue many lines of thought, she will do this in a *trained* way, not merely as an expression of petulant changefulness. She can even go to the extreme of being pugnacious and cross. She can have moods of depression and feelings of inadequacy and timidity about life, but she is stalwart and brave and will take a responsibility or a burden when it comes to her, as it undoubtedly will, and, as I said, in relation to one of her parents.

In spite of her pronounced " stickability," she can go off at a tangent and upset all calculations, suddenly changing her mind in an autocratic way.

She can have moody reckless moments when she hates all authority and control, yet she *likes* order *in her way* ! This child cannot possibly be " ordinary " so she must be helped to be un-ordinary in a suitable way. It may well be that if this is successful, she will find some line in which she will be quite outstanding.

She has charm and wit to help her and a good background.

In her relations with others, she can be cool, detached and with strong desire to be emotionally free, yet, in the background, she is loving and can even be possessive about things and people who mean a great deal to her. She can be sharp in speech but she must be trained not to be caustic but to use this gift of speech as quick-witted repartee and clever conversational ability.

With all that has been said about her, she has one splendid corrective, which is a gay, cheerful, pleasant way of behaving which helps her to ride over everything. She will attract opportunities to herself in life and take them easily and have a good share of " luck." You will remember that I said that even if anything went wrong with her, she would have the aptitude to turn it to good account !

She may not get all she wants in life as circumstances may hold her back and make her think and reflect but this will deepen her nature.

In her love affairs she will be gay but a little off hand. Her contradictoriness will be very evident as she is likely to rush towards whatever and whoever amuses her, then as suddenly retract and change her mind. She will have this attitude towards games, interests, and friends.

♀ ruler 7th
dispositor of
Satellitium,
♂ ☉ (by O–D)
♃, ruler 9th benasp
♑ M.C.

Strength in
♒ and ♉

☉ p ⊼ ♇
☿ p ♂ ☽
△ ♃
☿ ♂ ☉
(by O.D.)

T ♅ into 4th
T ♄ △ ☽♀♃ ☉
T ♃ ♂ Asc.

♂ p (ruler) has
left ♂ ♄ r
Ruler in ♉
♂ ♄

☿ p △ ♃ p
Asc. p♂ ♂
□ ☿
T ♂ ♂ Asc.
T ♃ ♂ ♂, ruler
and through 1st
☽ p Ⅱ — ♋

☿ p still △ ♃ P
♂ p closes □ ☉

She may marry or become engaged when about 18 years old.

She will have a strong urge to get around and abroad and to study interesting unusual subjects. As life goes on, she is likely to become more steadily ambitious but in her own unusual way.

Anything scientific, especially if to do with photography, light waves, radio, anything vibrational such as radionics will interest her. As a suggestion, her voice could be trained so that she would be a very perfect broadcaster.

1951

At the moment, she is in a mood which I tried to describe as " wanting to get rid of " so her own phrase of " having gone stale " on the school where she is, fits excellently. There is also an indication of improvement in her mental development.

1952

As the year develops, there is an indication of change in the home and more seriousness about work and also of mental expansion, all of which goes with a further indication of improved health and stability. It is interesting that I should know the school you had heard of and agree that it is just the school for a child who is not to be expected to allow herself to be moulded into a pattern.

The urgent thing of the moment seems to be that she should not have the great disadvantage of arriving there handicapped by poor reading and writing. The suggestion then is that steps should be taken as quickly as possible to get a really good young governess who specialises in coaching and to let her carry on Alicia's education at home till she can go to school when she is ten.

It should be explained to her firmly that this is her job in life for the next six months and that if she does not accomplish it, she will not be able to go to the new school. The change of tuition will probably produce a sudden flash of understanding and she will read and write well in a short time. Her mind is splendid and it is only this trait of being a " slow-starter " that has held her back.

1953

She seems to be even more energetic than usual and to throw herself into things with rashness and impetuosity. She may get feverish complaints at this time. She will be very mobile and changeful but she seems to have an added affection for and nearness to you.

1954

This is another good year, both for health and personal success. Her forcefulness becomes assertive. She must try to consider others before herself.

1955

Asc. p ☌ ♄

She must not overdo herself. For some reason, perhaps health, it appears that she has to moderate her enthusiasms a little, which is just as well. She will be 13 so her physical development may take some adjusting and she will have to accustom herself to it.

As you know, the calculations are made for years ahead and a discussion about Alicia can be arranged at any time. The way ahead for the moment seems clear and I hope she will have every success in her new life.

Comment from Mother

In 1952, in a telephone conversation, Alicia's mother said that it had been found that the school had its own arrangements for coaching new pupils, thus taking the place of the governess as suggested. The decision had been taken and Alicia was at school, happy when there but always hating the moment of leaving home.

She also said how much she wished she had been in possession of an astro-analysis of her daughter in earlier years as she now understood the difficulties in bringing her up.

In 1953, she wrote " I have always known that Alicia was a complex character but the analysis has helped me to see why, and that she was being pulled in two directions, sometimes being such a charming child and yet, in a few moments, being almost rude !

" Her Headmistress has recently told me Alicia's group had done a play in which she took the leading part and completely surprised them all by her performance, so much so that she felt she must let me know how outstanding it was. I wondered whether this was the beginning of the ' use of the voice ' that you mentioned."

CHAPTER 8

SHORT REPORT ON CONSULTATION

Chart C.—Mrs. B.

Reason for Inclusion

THE chart provides an interesting study because of its very definite shaping. Five planets are in a mutable cross, while two of these combine with another, Mars, to make a T-square, this other being highly important, because it not only combines these two formations, but is also the centre of a strong fan position. It rules 10th and 3rd.

From the point of view of interpretation, it is a good example of forwards astrology used in ordinary practice, the method being to make the usual systematic notes beforehand in readiness for full discussion by interview. By this means, an understanding then builds up between client and astrologer, the interpretation being further unfolded as its application to the life is revealed. After this, the report which is sent is more than just a piece of writing ; it is a reminder of the discussions on the main points as they emerged, these being of more value than an all-round-the-houses interpretation which must necessarily include many unwanted generalisations.

Case-history

This lady was known to be of good family and social background, happily married and in sympathy with projects in which her husband was interested. She asked " Am I essentially a ' fitter-in ' and a natural partner or mate ? Or is there a strong drive to stand on my own feet and build my own work and receive the responsibility and recognition that comes with it ? If this latter drive is sufficiently strong, then too much willingness to adjust myself to my husband will not agree with me in the long run and then, in the end, I'll be a poor partner as well." She asked for a general interpretation of her chart with an account of the tendencies at work in her life in the near future as she was considering putting her husband's projects to practical use.

First impressions

The shaping of the chart (mutable cross and T-square) was a surprise, since it showed a life of far more difficulty than would have been judged from a personal meeting, this being verified by the client at the interview. She knew a little astrology ; enough to be interested in this and other points.

The next impression was of the true way in which it showed the reason for her question since the Libran Sun and Mercury in the 8th (that which one shares with or gets from others in close connection) showed her sense of fitting-in, while her Aquarian ruler in Sagittarius showed her feeling for independence, her need being to combine the two attitudes by the use of the energy of the strongly placed and strongly aspected Mars, ruler of 3rd and 10th, the Saturn contacts giving the willingness to accept responsibility.

BIRTH CHART

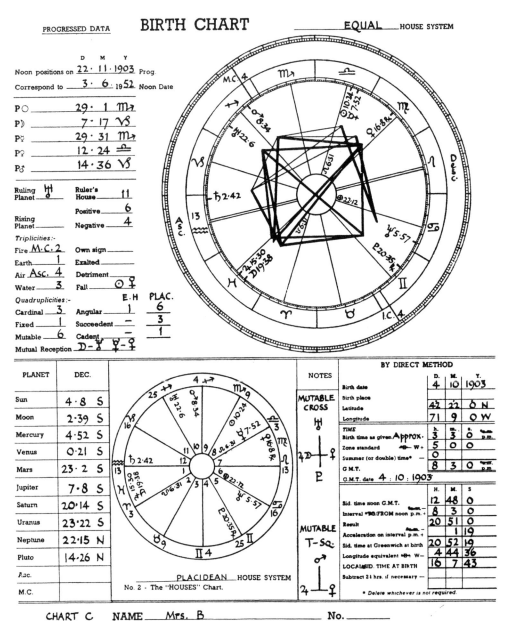

PROGRESSED DATA

EQUAL HOUSE SYSTEM

	D	M	Y
Noon positions on	22 · 11 · 1903 Prog.		
Correspond to	3 · 6 · 1952 Noon Date		

P☉	29 · 1 ♍
P☽	7 · 17 ♑
P☿	29 · 31 ♍
P♀	12 · 24 ♎
P♂	14 · 36 ♑

Ruling Planet ♅　　Ruler's House　11

Positive　6

Rising Planet ____　Negative　4

Triplicities:-

Fire M.C. 2　Own sign ____

Earth 1　Exalted ____

Air Asc. 4　Detriment ____

Water 3　Fall ☉ ☿

Quadruplicities:-　　　E.H　PLAC.

Cardinal 3　Angular 1　6

Fixed 1　Succeedent __　3

Mutable 6　Cadent __　1

Mutual Reception ☽-♂ ☿-♀

PLANET	DEC.
Sun	4·8 S
Moon	2·39 S
Mercury	4·52 S
Venus	0·21 S
Mars	23·2 S
Jupiter	7·8 S
Saturn	20·14 S
Uranus	23·22 S
Neptune	22·15 N
Pluto	14·26 N
Asc.	
M.C.	

PLACIDEAN HOUSE SYSTEM

No. 2 - The "HOUSES" Chart.

NOTES

MUTABLE CROSS ♅

2 D ___ ♀

P

MUTABLE T-Sq. ♂

2↓ ___ ♀

BY DIRECT METHOD

	D.	M.	Y.
Birth date	4	10	1903
Birth place			
Latitude	42	22	0 N
Longitude	71	9	0 W
TIME	h.	m.	s.
Birth time as given Approx.	3	3	0 p.m.
Zone standard ← W+	5	0	0
Summer (or double) time*	0		
G.M.T.	8	3	0 p.m.
G.M.T. date 4 : 10 : 1903			

	H.	M.	S
Sid. time noon G.M.T.	12	48	0
Interval TO/FROM noon p.m. +	8	3	0
Result	20	51	0
Acceleration on interval p.m. +		1	19
Sid. time at Greenwich at birth	20	52	19
Longitude equivalent ← W—	4	44	36
LOCAL SID. TIME AT BIRTH	16	7	43
Subtract 24 hrs. if necessary —			

* Delete whichever is not required.

CHART C　NAME Mrs. B　　　　No. _____

No. 1 - The "ECLIPTIC" Chart. DIRECT METHOD

Designed by M.E.HONE.

REPORT ON CONSULTATION*

Significators†

You will observe that the good old word, " horoscope," does not appear. It has been somewhat altered in meaning when applied to short paragraphs of interpretations for general reading. Moreover, the modern interest in astrology by educated people is not as an end in itself but as a technique by which to reach a desired end, which is the unbiased assessment of a human being from an examination of the situation of the ecliptic and the moving bodies in it at the time when that being entered the hemisphere in which he was born.

At this moment, one definite degree of ecliptic also entered it, rising over the eastern horizon. It is with this degree that he is aligned for his whole life. For you, the degree itself is not precisely known, since the exact moment of birth was not recorded, but it has been arrived at, by other astrologers, by calculation from subsequent events. Since the number of degrees from the M.C. to Uranus is 18 and since you say that no particular change occurred at this age, in fact, no special change till marriage at 22, I would be more inclined to think the M.C. could be 0° Sagittarius, giving an Asc. of 9° Aquarius. However, such exactitude does not matter except for the consideration of future events, in the calculation of which the precise degrees would be necessary.

By O-D
M.C. to ♅ ☌
at age 22‡

You will remember that I first read to you my short, curtly worded descriptive phrases, written deductively before you came, based on the main shaping of the chart, the outstanding points being the mutable cross, the extra T-square involving Mars, the inclusion of Asc.-ruler *and* Sun-ruler in this, in relation to the houses so combined, all being so strongly connected with the feelings (houses 2, 5, 8, 11).

Mutable +
T -sq.
Fan

My short paragraph from this was :—
" Here is a woman with many difficulties in life, many of which come to her from personal reasons, because of her feelings, and because she is, in the main, highly intelligent, yet with strong intuitive power and deep emotions."

Mutable +

+ involves
2nd, 5th, 8th, 11th
Asc. ♒
☽ ♃ in ♓
Full 8th

This you explained by telling of the difficulties and stresses you had gone through in totally different ways as results of your first two marriages, and your responsibility over bringing up the children.

---

* Notes and fore-pages omitted to save space.

† Significators entered on astrologer's carbon copy only.

‡ If the Ascendant is found to be either in the last degrees of one sign or the early degrees of another, then by careful questioning, it is advisable to try to decide which is the more suitable so that the ruling planet may be postulated. If there is no such uncertainty, and no urgent necessity to try to find the possible year of some event, then it is better to leave a chart as it is (especially as, in this case, it was said to be rectified already), saying that the birth is *about* the time given, pointing out that no deductions as to timing of tendencies in the life have been made from directions to or from the Asc. and M.C. ; these being nothing but surmise unless correct astronomical calculation from accurate birth-time has been possible.

⊙ ♎
☽ ♓
Asc. ♒

It was then expanded by showing that, while you were, what you called a good fitter-in (Libra) and with fine intuition (Pisces) yet the basic thing about you was your cool, detached, almost scientific attitude, which made you one who would, even in emotional stress, stand back and survey the matter on hand with a dispassionate *mental* assessment.

It was made clear that the custom in astrology in this country is to speak of the planet ruling the Ascendant as the main ruler of the map. Hence, though the sign-placing of Uranus is not always of strong importance, since this planet occupies a sign for seven years, *to you* it is of the greatest importance that it is in Sagittarius because it is your ruler.

♅ ruler
in ♐
⊙ ♎
☽ ♓

So, however much you embody the good-companion-ness of Libra and the quick sympathy of Pisces (your Sun and Moon signs), yet the core of you needs to be assured of its freedom, in ways which we alluded to as " geographical and mental." You *must* have scope to expand in the

♅ ruler in 11th

pursuit of your chosen objectives (Uranus, ruler in 11th), and you *must* feel free to be yourself in your own way.

Mutable +
in 2nd, 5th, 8th,
11th

From the houses involved and the extreme importance of the elevated and strongly aspected Mars, the deduction was given that the whole question of " contacts " in life, both of friends, acquaintances, husbands and children, had been a most complicated one.

♎ and ♓
strongly tenanted

Dealing next with the Ascendant and its close Saturn (which would be in orbs of conjunction if Asc. 9°), with the occupancy of Libra and Pisces, the next remarks were somewhat in the following vein : basically you are coolly observant, mentally weighing up circumstances and people with a quiet reserve, but also with a gentle understanding, and if necessary a sympathetic love and a desire to express this in your closer contacts in life. The desire is there but in none of these is there complete satisfaction, but rather it would be more true to say that the potentiality for this constantly urges you on to find it more and more fully.

Planets connected
by compulsive
aspects

♄ near Asc.
♄ rules 12th

For a woman, you are serious, having a pronounced sense of responsibility, especially for those whom you love. This is a deep drive from the unconscious. At bottom, you must have order and shape and this must be satisfied by the attempt to fulfil strong aspiration towards practical ideals. (Here you told of the burdens and stresses put on you in life in connection with your children and with the illness of the one child and then of the second husband, you being compulsively pressed into a serious view of life and aspirations, not only to do what you were called upon to do at those times, but to reshape your life in a better way, when you could.)

♆ and ♇ in 5th
malasp

⊙ ♎
✶ ♂

Every attribute of the Libran Sun is yours : looks, charm, suavity, harmony expressed in manner and appearance and the lovely ready smile which lights up the face so often. For you, life *must* contain harmony. You must find this in people around you, in furnishings, in

Ruler of 5th
in ♎

♃ ☌ ☽
in ♓

♎ and ♓
tenanted

♃ ☽ in ♓

☉ ☿ □ ♆
in ♋ in 5th
♇ ☍ ♅ in 11th
☉ ☿ ⚹ ♂
♄ near Asc.

☽ ☌ ♃ in 2nd
malasp

♃ ☽ ☍ ♀
□ ♂
□ ♇ in 5th

♀ □ ♂
wide, but
☍ ☽ ♃ □ ♇

♅, ruler
malasp

♅ ruler in 11th

⊕ 6th

♄ in 12th
benasp

atmosphere engendered by thoughts and pursuits, in colour, in line and in shape and in creative work.

To this you add the accentuated Piscean indication which gives you the warm intuition, the capability to be an open channel, to be impressionable to what comes to you in those unexplainable ways which we discussed at length in relation to other mutual interests.

These are not only of the mediumistic type but include the necessary inspiration before any work of art, or poem can be conceived, or even the formulation of the theory of the scientist which he will then labour to prove by reason. This brings you also to a love of rhythm in all its many manifestations, rhythm in the dance, in the waves of the sea, and in colour sequences. We noted that with strongly accented Libra and Pisces, you love sailing which brings you beauty, colour, changing moods of the weather and the thrill of rhythmic movement.

Unfortunately, it had to be remarked that though physically and mentally there was robust intent to reach extremely high ideals, there must have been and always would be much difficulty of accomplishment, much hindrance and delay in objectives and much need for the patience and acceptance of responsibility spoken of earlier.

Other points commented on were :—

1. A generosity about money and a certain amount of good fortune in the circumstances but not always as required.

2. A certain harshness in the life, due to difficulties against which a fight had to be made, thus bringing pugnacity into being which toughened the fibre, causing also what I described as " a jettisoning of certain ideals and joys." (We never read this paragraph in the notes but how well it agrees with what you described in having to give second place to your creative work because of the need to be available for your sick boy !)

In this part of the notes was also a phrase unread, commenting on the fact that at times the difficulties had not been helpful towards happiness in sex life, but that you had developed a genius for companionship which is a most rewarding thing.

3. Change, as an ingredient of life, was described as so much a part of your life that you are conditioned to it, so that it is of less consequence to you than a small alteration would be to a person more statically placed. Also that journeys were likely to be in pursuit of an objective. (*Not* because I knew the reasons for your repeated journeys to various countries but as a plain translation of Uranus, Asc.-ruler, in Sagittarius, in 11th house.)

4. Work was referred to as a pleasurable thing so long as it could be sensed as for the good of others, or for a cause or objective. Another comment which remained unread was that the most satisfaction in life would come, not through the lighter pleasures, but through concentration, achievement over difficulties and through all those things

Full 8th
♄ 12th
rules 12th

which are not public or on the surface of life. This includes such different things as the deeper emotional happinesses of married life, and the interest in work for others in quiet ways, and in connection with occult matters or those not generally noticed by the public.

☽, rules 6th
malasp
☽ ☌ ♃

5. Health was not fully discussed except to comment that the obvious troubles inherent in the difficult aspects of its significator in your chart (Moon, ruler 6th) were much mitigated so that you would come out on the right side when anything went wrong (conjunction Jupiter).

PRESENT TIME
1952

⊙ p ☌ ☿ p
both 29 ♏
♀ p ∟ ♂
(natal trine)

This is a year of deep-seated psychological change. (Sun and Mercury about to progress from Scorpio to Sagittarius.) Henceforward life should contain a little less emotion, less tensity, less hurt feelings and a period should begin in which there is more free-ranging activity both of mind and body. *Both* must be left free and independent to roam when the desire to be alone is strong. There should be time for travel, investigation, optimistic philosophical mental work. There is likely to be connection with writing and publishing. The year should also be characterised as a time of great idealism, of risk-taking, of more interest in those rhythmic things which manifest as art, music and dance.

by O-D
♀ △ ♆

Important Note.—As the degree of M.C. is not certain, a very definite effect on the career in the near future cannot be accurately timed. If the chart is correct as it stands, then the results of this change of inner direction should show in outward arrangements and activities *in four years time*. If, however, the possible alteration suggested is correct, then such plans should materialise within the next few months.

⊙ p to M.C.

1953

(Since the following paragraph as written in my notes is so amply descriptive of possible activities which you have now outlined, it would seem more interesting to you if quoted just as it is. For your astrological friend's interest, it should be noted that the deductions are by a newly conceived theory to do with the relationship between the cusp of 10th house in Equal House Division and the degree of M.C. used as cusp 10 in divisions by quadrant systems.)*

♂ p ruler 10th E.H.
enters 12th
⚹ ♃ ruler 12th
in ♓ in 2nd

♏ on 10th

" This year brings an accentuation of assertive, initiatory, business-like activity, possibly entailing argument or more serious disagreements, involving financial considerations. This has to do with matters either secret to the self, *or* to do with retired work such as connected with hospitals and so on. Some project, perhaps for healing, dear to the heart, now brought to functioning."

* Discussed in Chapter 13.

Spring and Summer

T ♇ △ ♅ ruler
from 7th to 10th

"New phase *to* self *from* husband." (This was the very short wording but it may be misunderstood. It carries a meaning that the newness which is expected strongly affects the self, but very specially as a result of, or through, the husband.) "There is also a connection with ' children,' these being actual or of the mind and the imagination.

(♇ in natal 5th)

♇ ☍ ♅ (natal)
but ♅ ruler
involved in
mutable +
Transits of ♃ and ♅

"This whole process of growth is *not* easy, but the life is conditioned to kicking out and prodding for what the mind wants. In spite of various obstructions, the summer is the time of greatest opportunities."

DETAILS OF 1952-3

(The minor tendencies for this time are not strongly marked, but some remarks may be of interest.)

☽ p ♑

In general : The mood is towards what might be described as " shaping and forming."

T ♄ △ ♇
T ♃ △ ♀
T ♂ ☌ ♄

November

A happily busy time especially at the end.

January
19th–24th

T ♅ △ ♃ in 2nd
T ♂ ☌ ♃ in 2nd
T ♂ ☌ ☽, ruler 6th

This is the most marked time. There is likely to be increased expenditure and it would be as well to be thoughtful and not rash. Also the health should not be neglected just now.

February–July

Long transit
of ♇ △ ♅ and
of ♅ △ ♃ ☽ 2nd

No ♄ transits
T ♂ ☌ ♇ Ψ

This whole period is characterised as a time of personal change and the start of one of the many " new phases " in life. The general effect on money and possessions should be good.

Within the period mentioned, there is little frustration or delay. Towards the end both of May and of June, there are upsetting moments, probably connected with your children. Other than that, there is a close succession of transits by Jupiter from May to September. As the natal planets are in so close a square, it would be unwise to hazard an opinion as to the effects to be noted in relation to this, without much more experience of the previous working of this in the life.

T ♃ △ ♄
    △ ☿
    △ ☉

Beneficial times can be stated to be :—
18th May, 11th June, 23rd June.

1954

☉ p ∟ ♂ p
♂ p △ ♀ r
☿ p ⚹ ♄ r
☽ p ☌ ♄
    then ☌ Asc.

Much concentration on job on hand. Combative and urgent spirit shown. Very much more happiness in life with those nearest. Attraction becomes stronger. Mental outlook is towards serious matters, but towards a chosen end with good result long awaited.

☉ p ✱ ♄ in 12th
☿ p ☌ M.C.
(if correct)
✱ ♄ p
T ♃ △ M.C.
△ ♅

1955

A time of settlement, of arriving at a goal. This applies more to things not on the surface and not materialistic. Even so, social life, business interests, outward matters combine well with home affairs.

☽ p ♒
sign of Asc.

1956

Superficial tendencies come more into line with main basic trends, thus bringing satisfaction.

Extracts from Client's Letter to Astrologer

"You are correct about my chart. I'll jot down some comments as I look over your report. The paragraph which begins 'Here is a woman with many difficulties in life' is correct. I could have lived an easier life if strong emotions and intuitions had not carried me from my parents' environment and into the thick of things ; also I do try very hard, even when much involved emotionally, to keep at least a little section of myself objective.

"About your paragraph on Uranus, my ruler, in Sagittarius. It is correct that 'the core' of me 'needs to be assured of freedom' only that is too mild ! It *insists* on freedom ! That was my difficulty for quite a while ; I couldn't marry because I couldn't find a man who didn't seem hedged in his point of view.

"As regards 'change, as an ingredient of life,' I feel as if I had lived several lives in one, it has been so varied.

"In regard to the paragraph about sympathy ; I like to be understanding and helpful but am unsure how far to go in this and therefore you are right about not finding this quality very satisfying. The next paragraph is also correct.

"Sun in Libra. Yes, I always seek to make or find harmony and think that has been my chief satisfaction.

"The paragraph about accentuated Pisces is good as I am most happy when using intuition or rhythm in various forms but I want to add 'when being creative or making things happen.' This is not from Pisces, I suppose. [Note by M.E.H. : addition of ruler of Pisces in 5th.]

"Next paragraphs are correct. The difficulties about happiness in sex life were true in earlier days. 'Change' ; yes, I like it and like to meet new challenges. Note 4 on work but I want to know what shows it in my chart. [Note by M.E.H. See marginal significators.] This paragraph answers the question I had in mind when I came to you about my ability to combine freedom with partnership.

"From your report, it looks as if I have the necessary ingredients to do this, also circumstances look more and more favourable, so I am feeling happy and optimistic. I do recognise this time (1952–3) as one of new beginning. I know I have ability to make changes and I enjoy change as something new."

Note.—In case readers have not read similar notes in other chapters, it should be repeated that the writer regrets if an impression is given of showing her own correctness. She wishes to show the *correctness of astrological interpretation* and can only do so by publishing such confirmations for which kind permission has been given.

CHAPTER 9

ASTRO-ANALYSIS FOR A CLIENT UNDERSTANDING ASTROLOGICAL TERMINOLOGY

Chart D—A BUSINESS WOMAN

Reason for Inclusion

As the writer has so constantly stressed the opinion that the average member of the public feels nothing but irritation at the inclusion, in a character analysis, of astrological terms which are completely unintelligible to him, it is a variation to include one written in answer to definite questions from the client who has a certain amount of astrological knowledge. This correspondent's own confirmatory letters add interest to the chapter.

Case History

" At the moment I have two businesses. 1. School Counsellor which I have founded and run since 1933. This means that I help parents to find schools for their children. 2. Export and Import business of my father which came to me when my brother was killed suddenly on 1st February, 1950 (his 52nd birthday). I bought out my sister-in-law. My question is how am I going to get along in the year 1952/3? Do the aspects look favourable towards my reorganising the export business and putting it on its feet financially? Also, I have an amateur's interest in astrology and would like to know what you think will be the effect of the conjunction of Saturn and Neptune on my natal Mercury? "

First Impressions on the Chart

(Full notes as usual written later.)

It is of interest to note that Mars, her Sun-ruler, is very importantly placed, since it is in 10th, near M.C. in good aspect to Mercury in 2nd, this being ruler of her Asc. *and* M.C. Moreover it is in a dual sign and she now has two businesses. Naturally, *every* Virgo has the nonagesimal in Gemini but not all will have the M.C. also, nor will all have the Sun-ruler working in the mode of that sign. Her professions are unusual. This shows the fatuity of thinking that an astrologer should be able to tell the profession precisely from the chart. What *can* be told is that it is likely to be something *in the nature of* Mercury, but the end-result may be one of many. Mercury's house-position and rulerships are especially important this year and next (1952/3) in view of the recurring Saturn-Neptune conjunction in the degree it occupies. It has added significance as the dispositor of Jupiter and Mars and the usual Neptune-Pluto conjunction common to all born in the same decade.

ASTRO-ANALYSIS*

Significators†

Asc. earth
☉ water
✳ ♃

Your character is an extremely interesting mixture of forthright common sense and practicality with a streak of ability to get ideas intuitively rather than rationally, plus a slice of good fortune which enables you to " pull off " an enterprise where another person might not be successful.

* Notes and fore-pages omitted to save space.
† Significators entered on astrologer's carbon copy only.

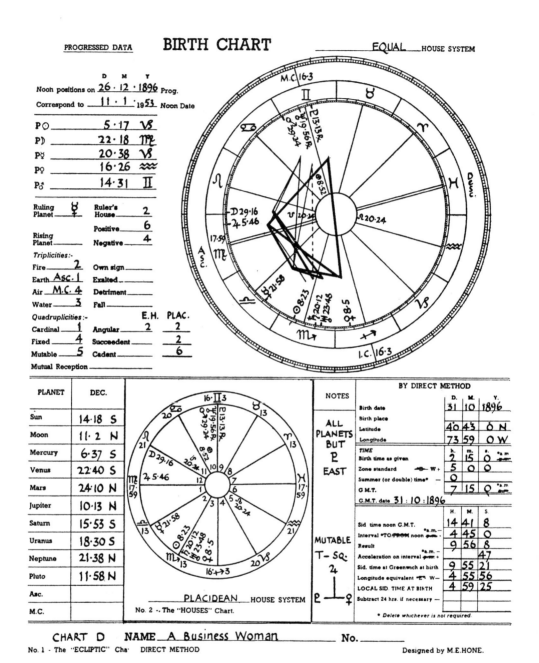

BIRTH CHART

PROGRESSED DATA   EQUAL HOUSE SYSTEM

	D	M	Y	
Noon positions on	26 · 12 · 1896	Prog.		
Correspond to	11 · 1 · 1953	Noon Date		

P☉	5·17	♑
P☽	22·18	♍
P☿	20·38	♑
P♀	16·26	♒
P♂	14·31	♊

Ruling Planet	☿	Ruler's House	2	
		Positive	6	
Rising Planet		Negative	4	

Triplicities:-

Fire	2	Own sign	
Earth	Asc. 1	Exalted	
Air	M.C. 4	Detriment	
Water	3	Fall	

Quadruplicities:-

			E.H.	PLAC.
Cardinal	1	Angular	2	2
Fixed	4	Succeedent		2
Mutable	5	Cadent		6
Mutual Reception				

M.C. 16·3

Desc.

Asc. ♍

I.C. 16·3

PLANET	DEC.
Sun	14·18 S
Moon	11·2 N
Mercury	6·37 S
Venus	22·40 S
Mars	24·10 N
Jupiter	10·13 N
Saturn	15·53 S
Uranus	18·30 S
Neptune	21·38 N
Pluto	11·58 N
Asc.	
M.C.	

NOTES

ALL PLANETS BUT ♇ EAST

MUTABLE T- SQ. ♃ ⊥ ♇ — ♀

PLACIDEAN HOUSE SYSTEM

No. 2 - The "HOUSES" Chart.

BY DIRECT METHOD

	D.	M.	Y.
Birth date	31	10	1896
Birth place			
Latitude	40·43		0 N
Longitude	73·59		0 W

TIME	h.	m.	s.
Birth time as given	2	15	0 a.m.
Zone standard W +	5	0	0
Summer (or double) time°	0		
G.M.T.	7	15	0 a.m
G.M.T. date 31 : 10 : 1896			

	H.	M.	S.
Sid time noon G.M.T. a.m.	14	41	8
Interval °TO/FROM noon p.m.	4	45	0
Result a.m.	9	56	8
Acceleration on interval p.m. +			47
Sid. time at Greenwich at birth	9	55	21
Longitude equivalent °E W—	4	55	56
LOCAL SID. TIME AT BIRTH	4	59	25
Subtract 24 hrs. if necessary —			

° Delete whichever is not required.

CHART D   NAME A Business Woman   No._____

No. 1 - The "ECLIPTIC" Chart DIRECT METHOD   Designed by M.E.HONE.

Most planets on east
Ruler in 2nd
☉ in 2nd

Your life as you describe it, is perfect in its way of giving expression to your most outstanding traits. Firstly, you are essentially a woman who is able to carve out her own path in life. Next, you are definitely particularly interested in making money and able to use your whole personality in so doing. Being an intelligent and educated person, you would want to deal with affairs which need such ability, yet, being capable of quick and intense feeling, you would prefer a life in which the personal element counts. Hence, you are successful in suiting the tastes of your clients because you study each one's different requirements.

♄ in 3rd

It would seem that you did not have too good a start educationally or that things were made difficult for you so it is all the more to your credit that you have forged your own way through.

Asc. ♍

With your Virgo Ascendant, you must have a strong and well developed sense of detail and a desire to help others. You would naturally like to be a " go-between." So, in careful looking into the running of the different schools and assessing them with a critical eye for the sake of your clients, you are using the well-known Virgo discrimination for a good purpose. This is an excellent thing because, as you probably know, many a Virgo makes herself disliked by being too critical of other people and is thought interfering when she notices and points out details which would escape a less sharp eye. By being in a profession which uses this to good effect, you are more likely to sit back in leisure hours and restfully let details go by without comment, thus becoming a more popular person yourself.

☿ △ ♆ in 10th
△ ♂ in 10th
⚺ ♄ ♅

In all your dealings in life, you have high ideals for your standing and your prestige in the world, so you put considerable energy into whatever you decide to do. Had you not taken up this special career, you could have written, lectured or taught in whatever subject had interested you. This could well have been on the medical or scientific side. Hygiene and health interest you, since you have a sense of purity

☿ ⚺ ♅ in 3rd

and cleanliness ; this can be true in actuality and also figuratively speaking.

♂ △ ☿
⚹ ♃
⚹ ☽

You would be a tireless worker, constantly adding more to that which you have set yourself to do. Your new interest in buying and selling is again a typically Mercurian occupation as " go-between." In this case, between wholesaler and client.

☿ ∟ ♃ in 12th

This readiness to increase may develop into an exaggeration or an overdoing if not wisely controlled. You have a strong unconscious urge to do things in a big way, in fact a strong drive to success but this can affect your health if care is not taken.

Asc. ♍

The question of health is closely wrapped up with your mental attitude. Once you have realised this, you will allow for it and restrict yourself with intelligent self-direction. For you, worry is a poison. Worry comes because you cannot help but see fine points which another

☽ ♌

☿ ∠ ♀ in 3rd

would pass by. Worry can react on your nerves, particularly the nerves of your stomach and intestines, and could cause indigestion and also tendency to duodenal and gastric ulcers. You can control this to a certain extent by using your very good organising ability so that you plan your time and your work and get plenty of rest and relaxation. Worry over details can also affect the pleasures of social life and the companionship of loved ones, both in the family and out of it.

☉ ♏ 2nd
Exact ⚺ ♀
⚹ ♃
☉ ⚺ ♀

In your relations with others, your feelings can be deep and intense and also penetrative in regard to their feelings for you. You can be jealous and even possessive where you love but your natural charm of manner and habitual pleasantness of speech would prevent you from showing it. Socially, you would be cheerful and convivial. When necessary, your manner can be dignified and almost autocratic.

☽ ♌ 12th
ben-mal
⚹ ♂
□ ♄
□ ♅ in 3rd

Occasionally you can have moods of deep depression and there are times when it is not easy to control a rush of hasty, rebellious, irritated emotion that surges to the surface and may break out into speech. Fortunately, there is so much natural suavity that control is generally used, since it is realised that it is not only more pleasant but more expedient to control too much expression. Even so, undercurrents of hurt feelings can be left to cause depression. If possible, this should always be rooted out, since it is such brooding which affects digestion. It may be caused by family affairs or by upsets with neighbours who become uncongenial.

♄ in ♏ in 3rd
♅ in ♏ in 3rd
malasp

Your buying out your brother's business is well shown in your chart as a predisposition to find responsibility through the affairs of a brother. Your relations with him could have been unusual in some way and not always without difficulties.

♓ 7th

Asc. ♍

If you marry, it is likely to be out of a feeling of desire to help someone, knowing that he needs you. To such a partner, you would be full of sympathy and always ready with the kindly, helpful action in any way required, in fact always looking ahead to see what preparations could be made to help life to be happier.

Present Time (1952–3)

☉ p △ ♃ (53)
☿ p ⚹ ♄ (53)
☽ p ♍ ☌ Asc.

In the main, this is a year of expansion and success which becomes more enjoyable in 1953. There are unavoidable moments of depression and anxiety and of feeling that responsibility is heavy. Work is arduous and pressing but is worth it in view of the undoubted success of next year.

☉ p △ ♃

Your main question was in relation to the prospects of the import–export business which you have taken over and it is the greatest pleasure to be able to assess these as *first-rate*.

Your natural tendency to grasp opportunities and profit by them, comes to its full flower this next year and you should see the budding of this in the next few months. There is no better augury for success than that shown in a chart in which the Sun is sextile to Jupiter at birth and then comes to the trine by progression ; this is what occurs in your chart next year and begins to be felt some months before. In your case, there should be excellent financial advantage, and, though in practical matters of commerce, there is strong indication that your success is partly through acting on initiative and impulse through your shrewd intuition. This should also affect your feelings bringing you not only happiness but a feeling of stability and settlement. Undoubtedly, you will have to give up something in other ways to achieve this. You will need to limit your pleasures and be somewhat single-minded in your objectives but you will not mind that. Your mood is towards an accentuation of that marked ability to watch the details of an undertaking, letting nothing slip.

You ask especially about the effect of *the Neptune–Saturn conjunction on your Mercury.* First you must consider that Mercury, in *your* chart, not only is significator of your mind and nervous system, but of yourself, since it is your ruler. It is extremely well aspected by trines to Mars and Neptune in your 10th house but forced into action by the semi-squares to Jupiter and Venus. Hence it is to be realised that the results of excellent and energetic business sense will be well affected by this conjunction, but also the tendency to overdo and overact will be aroused and so may upset relationships with others.

The Saturn principle must act in accordance with its nature, which is to impose limits, while the Neptune principle must also be true to itself in that it will seek to dissolve all limits and to impose a boundless and vague idealism, setting up an impressionability which can be subversive. Here are two utterly opposite principles or urges at work at the same time. Naturally, you will be distracted by this dual pull but far *less* distracted than you would be if you did not know about it. Instead of being vexed with yourself at what you might consider a weak changeability in moods and consequent decisions, you will now be standing back from yourself, so to speak, and being amused at the spectacle of yourself being completely practical and common-sense one day, yet with your head in the clouds the next day.

As the transitting conjunction affects you through the second house of your chart, you will need to be careful in monetary matters. If such a forceful transit occurred in any other year, you might indeed be apprehensive of difficulties ahead, but with the excellent trine of progressed Sun to Jupiter, you must come out on top.

It is necessary to ask you to be more than usually watchful of others who might not be as straight with you as they appear to be. Also it would be wise for you to expect and allow for some frustrations and also for delays. In a year's time, these should be seen as stabilisers which have done no harm, but, conversely, have done good in making you go carefully.

It is not quite easy for me to word my remarks to you. Usually, I do not introduce any astrological terminology into these analyses, unless I am sure that the reader will understand, and with you I am not sure just how much you do follow astrological reasoning. Do you understand if I tell you that, this year, you have also the excellent progressed aspect of Mercury sextile Saturn ? It is particularly good since the two are so closely united by semi-sextile at birth. This is an added testimony to stability and consolidation, this being another anchor to hold you against any drifting which might be suspected from the Neptune transit.

☿ p ⚹ ♄

DETAILS OF THE NEXT TWELVE MONTHS
1952–3

Main transits
interpreted in
relation to minor
transits

(In these minor remarks, none has been based on aspects or transits to Ascendant or Midheaven, since you are not exactly sure of the birth-time. Since you said " between two and two-thirty," the chart is calculated for two-fifteen, making these and the degree of the Moon slightly later than you gave them.)

August

T ♄ △ ♇

Things seem to start moving to some purpose. New ways open out.

10th to 17th

T ♂ ☌ ♄ ♅

Care should be taken not to allow remarks to be sharp or cutting ; also that rashness in every way is moderated.

18th

T ♃ ☍ ♄

From now until the end of September, overdoing and over-worrying must be watched.

September
1st

T ♆ △ ♆

Around this time, your mind should be most fertile of good ideas, advantageous in business but be careful to put them into practice and not just dream them.

10th

T ♂ ☌ ♀

Be extremely careful in all relationships with others. Avoid any argumentativeness.

October
27th to 28th

T ♄ △ ♆
T ♆ ☌ ☿

On these two days you have the first transit of Neptune over your Mercury with Saturn trine your Neptune. This must be combined with the next paragraph. See November.

November
13th

T ♄ ☌ ☿

On this day you have the transit of Saturn moving on to the Mercury. *Nowadays these are taken as multiple transits affecting a period, rather than as indications of happenings on special days.* Be careful as already outlined. Treat the whole period with care, seeing that you do not allow yourself to become either depressed or in any way careless. Take a long view and think of the excellent backing of aspects which are far more important than transits.

December
The effect continues mildly.

January 1953
T ♇ □ ♅

New phases are likely to begin. New agreements may be necessary. Try not to be rushed into anything but take good advice and go slowly.

February
New Moon
□ ♅

There is still need for refusal to hurry into hasty decisions.

March
21st
T ♃ ☍ ♄

As in August (1952), take enough rest and don't overdo.

April
7th
T ♃ ☍ ♅

Too much to see to can affect your health. Insist on planned work with planned recreation.

May and June
Multiple T's
T ♄ ☌ ☿
T ♃ □ ☽ ♃
T ♂ ☌ ♇
T ♂ ☌ M.C. ♆
T ♆ ☌ ☿
T ♃ ☍ ♀
T ♂ ☌ ♂

Again, the two should be combined because of the combined Saturn-Neptune effect spread over the period. From more than one point of view, there is still the fear of overdoing what you set out to do. You will be extremely busy, especially from 18th May to 12th June. This latter date is an excellent one on which to get any enterprise *started*. You will be feeling especially energetic and assertive and ready to take a new step and you should now go ahead.

July
T ♅ △ ♄
T ♃ ☌ ♇
    ☌ M.C.
    □ Asc.

In the early part of the month (about the 6th), you should experience some desire to free yourself from a tie but you will find it difficult. It is more likely that the last few days of the month will be suddenly easier.

1954
♀ p ruler 2nd,
    P ♄ p
T ♄ ☌ ☉
T ♃ △ ☉
later

Aspects and transits are of very mixed natures. While financial matters should be easier in the spring, there will be personal frustrations, becoming easier in the autumn.

1955
☿ p ⚹ ♅
♀ p △ ♆ p
☽ p ☌ ☿

Basically very good indeed. There is likelihood of personal change perhaps by travel. There is a hint of more companionship in the life, more interest in art or music, more feeling for beauty and rhythm. Transits again are of very mixed natures, so while moods of depression arise, other happy and optimistic moments soon follow them.

☉ p ✱ ☉
☿ p □ ♃ p
♀ p △ ♆
□ ♄
☽ p ♏

1956

The softer, gentler, more intuitive mood increases, bringing you new pleasures and interests. Difficulties are mainly in the spring, improving in summer and autumn.

☿ p ✱ ♄ p
♀ p △ ☿

1957

Stability increases though it has been at some cost to mind and nerves, due to the long transit of Saturn over the five planets in Scorpio and Sagittarius. You will feel considerable relief when this is over as the year finishes. Both personal happiness and financial stability seem more secure by the end of the year.

☉ p △ ♃ p
♂ p ☌ ♇
☽ ↑ ☌ ♀
T 's good

1958

Though only five years should be surveyed for this reading, it must be continued for one more year because it should be a splendid year of rounding off whatever you have been doing. Transits are excellent and you should enjoy this year thoroughly.

Extracts from Client's Letters to Astrologer

" I am going to make a few comments on the analysis. I am interested in ' Virgoan, with Sun in Scorpio ' ; that seems to be me much more than just ' Scorpio.' You are right that I did not have too good a start educationally. The private schools I attended were considered excellent. But the education planned for me was changed because of World War I. I was supposed to have had my education in Europe and was in a Swiss school in Geneva when the war broke. I returned immediately to New York and insisted on going back to preparatory school to get ready to go to university the following year. As I was far from intellectual, it was a real effort. I enjoyed the life and the studies and the friends but I was far from an honour student.

" I'll take your advice and try not to drive myself. At the moment, it seems that I can't get the work done either by myself or with those who are there to help me. I'll also take your advice about not worrying because I know that everything you say is true. I was very ill from 1941–9 (though I never stopped work), an illness which took the form of poison coming out on my hands and feet. I found the cure in a combination of unorthodox remedies, diet and breathing and elimination—no drugs. (No, I'm not a fanatic !) I am fine now, but *can't worry or the thing flares up again.*

" When you say, ' Even so, undercurrents of hurt feelings can be left to cause depression,' you are so right. I am glad you brought out that so clearly because I think I have not made enough conscious effort to get rid of these undercurrents and have too often got my feelings hurt, both by my near relatives and neighbours when they seemed unfair, according to *my* code of fairness. With the advice you have given me, I shall hope to be able to cease being the recording angel and so shall cease to have my feelings hurt and thus escape my fits of depression.

" I have noted what you say about my reaction to marriage, should I marry. In an early time of my life I would have wanted to pursue this topic more, just now I feel that I have too much on my mind to be bothered by the time-consuming occupation of being in love. I have always felt that Pluto opposition Venus, both square Jupiter, has prevented me either meeting the right person or, having met the right person, some insurmountable hurdle has separated us. At the moment it isn't important to me, for which I am duly grateful."

CHAPTER 10

LOVE OR DUTY ?

Charts E, F, and G.—The Man, His Wife and " The Other "

Reasons for Inclusion

THE problem of the man–woman relationship is probably the most important thing in the lives of most people and the most frequent of the difficulties in which an astrologer is asked to help. As readers may realise, though stories of these cases are of the greatest human interest, their details are usually too private and too sad to be included in such a book as this.

In this instance, the man in question (an engineer with a well-known firm) by his own analysis of himself and his problem, contributed vividly to the whole discussion and, later on, agreed to reproduction of extracts from it. He knew enough astrology to wish for astrological reasoning to be given in explanation of what was written.

Another reason for the inclusion of this chart is that it is illustrative of those of many thousands of people all over the world born when Neptune and Uranus, in Cancer and Capricorn, were in opposition to each other five times owing to retrogradation. The times when this relationship was exact were May 1905, February 1907, July and December 1908 and September 1910. As both planets move slowly, the configuration was within orbs of conjunction for several weeks each time. Those born were young children in the 1914 war, subject to the upsets in homes from which the father went away. They were the adults who bore the brunt of the 1939 war, either as men in the forces or women trying to look after homes and do duty in Fire Brigade, Ambulance Service or fire-watching as well. No wonder the tense strain of this opposition has shown in their lives ! Those who have suffered most are of the times when (a) the opposition was made more difficult to bear by the addition of other planets, particularly their Suns or rulers, to the two ends of the opposition ; (b) the opposition was across the degrees of ecliptic crossed by horizon or meridian (Asc.-Desc. or M.C.-I.C.) ; (c) Saturn was in Aries, square both ends of the opposition.

Since 1949, Uranus in its passage through Cancer has affected all these by transit, coming to the conjunction to the Cancer planets, opposition to its own place and any other planets in Capricorn, squaring any in Aries or Libra. Any astrologer can produce charts of a succession of clients who have recently come to him with their difficulties under this transit, varying according to house position, and met in varying ways according to the Ascendant and the life-pattern as shown by the rest of the chart.

Now, in 1952–3, those with the later degrees occupied have not only the transit of Uranus alone but the multiple effect of the square from the conjunction of Saturn and Neptune in Libra. This again was made even more drastic when other more quickly moving planets were in Aries, Libra or Capricorn. These Cardinal squares have been indicative of many difficulties in personal and national life in these years and have marked most of the period of the two years as difficult for those " beginning moments " which are the foundations of all charts to be used astrologically.

BIRTH CHART

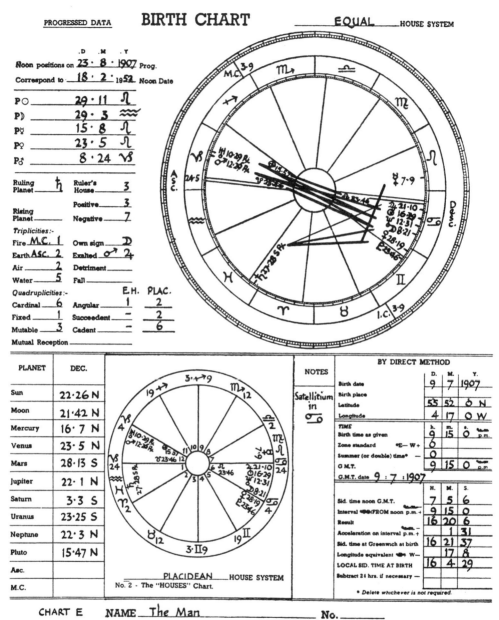

PROGRESSED DATA   **BIRTH CHART**   _____EQUAL_____ HOUSE SYSTEM

Noon positions on **23 · 8 · 1907** Prog.

Correspond to ___**18 · 2** · 19**52** Noon Date

P☉ _____ **29 · 11** ♌
P☽ _____ **29 · 3** ♒
P☿ _____ **15 · 8** ♌
P♀ _____ **23 · 5** ♌
P♂ _____ **8 · 24** ♑

Ruling Planet	♄	Ruler's House	3
		Positive	3
Rising Planet		Negative	7

Triplicities:-
Fire **M.C. 1**   Own sign **☽**
Earth **ASC. 2**   Exalted **♂ ♃**
Air ____ **2**   Detriment ____
Water ____ **5**   Fall ____

Quadruplicities:-   E.H.   PLAC.
Cardinal **6**   Angular **1**   **2**
Fixed **1**   Succeedent **-**   **2**
Mutable **3**   Cadent **-**   **6**
Mutual Reception ____

PLANET	DEC.
Sun	22·26 N
Moon	21·42 N
Mercury	16·7 N
Venus	23·5 N
Mars	28·13 S
Jupiter	22·1 N
Saturn	3·3 S
Uranus	23·25 S
Neptune	22·3 N
Pluto	15·47 N
Asc.	
M.C.	

PLACIDEAN HOUSE SYSTEM
No. 2 - The "HOUSES" Chart.

NOTES

Satellitium in ♋

		D.	M.	Y.
BY DIRECT METHOD				
Birth date		9	7	1907
Birth place				
Latitude		55	52	0 N
Longitude		4	17	0 W

TIME		h.	m.	s.
Birth time as given		9	15	0 p.m.
Zone standard ✱E — W+		0		
Summer (or double) time✱		0		
G.M.T.		9	15	0 p.m

G.M.T. date **9 : 7 : 1907**

	H.	M.	S.
Sid. time noon G.M.T.	7	5	6
Interval ✱✱/FROM noon p.m.+	9	15	0
Result	16	20	6
Acceleration on interval p.m.+		1	31
Sid. time at Greenwich at birth	16	21	37
Longitude equivalent ✱✱ W—		17	8
LOCAL SID. TIME AT BIRTH	16	4	29
Subtract 24 hrs. if necessary —			

✱ Delete whichever is not required.

CHART E   NAME **The Man**   No._____

No. 1 - The "ECLIPTIC" Chart. DIRECT METHOD

Designed by M.E.HONE.

FIVE YEAR SHEET

1952

☉	∟	♆	p	
♀	✶	♇		
	⊡	♂	p	
Asc.	△	♂		
♄	△	♂	} O–D	
☽	✶	♇		

☽ ♒– ♓

1953

	T ♆ △ ♇				Spring–autumn
		☐ ♃ Asc.			Summer–autumn
	T ♅ ☌ ☉				Jan. June
		☌ ♃			September
☉ enters ♍	T ♄ △ ♀				Autumn
♀ ⊼ Asc.	☽ ♓	T ♃ △ ♅ ♂			Spring
⊡ ♅ p		☌ ♇ ☐ ♄			Autumn

1954

	T ♆ △ ♇ ☐ Asc.		Summer
	T ♅ ☌ ♃		Jan. June
	☍ Asc.		August
	△ ♄		Autumn
☉ ⊻ ♃ p	T ♄ ☐ ☿		Spring–autumn
♀ ⊼ ♄ p	☽ ♓– ♈	△ ☽	Autumn
	△ ☉		Winter
	T ♃ ☌ ♇ ♀ ☐ ♄		Spring
	☌ ☽ ♆ ☉ ♃		Summer

1955

	T ♆ △ ♀		Autumn
	T ♅ ☍ Asc.		Spring
	△ ♄		Summer
♂ ☌ ♅ p	T ♄ △ ♃		Spring-autumn
♀ ⊼ ♄	☽ ♈	△ ☉	Summer
	△ ♄		Winter
	T ♃ ☌ ♃ △ ♄		Spring
	☌ ☿		Summer

1956

	T ♆ △ ♀		Autumn
	T ♅ ☌ ☿		Autumn
☉ ☐ M.C.	T ♄ ☌ M.C.		Spring–autumn
☿ ✶ ♇	☽ ♈– ♉	△ ♄	Summer–autumn
⊼ Asc.	△ ☿		Winter
♀ ✶ ♀	T ♃ ☐ M.C.		Summer
	△ ♂ ♅ Asc. ☍ ♄		Autumn
	☐ ♇ ♀		Winter

* See footnote below ten year sheet in Chapter 6.

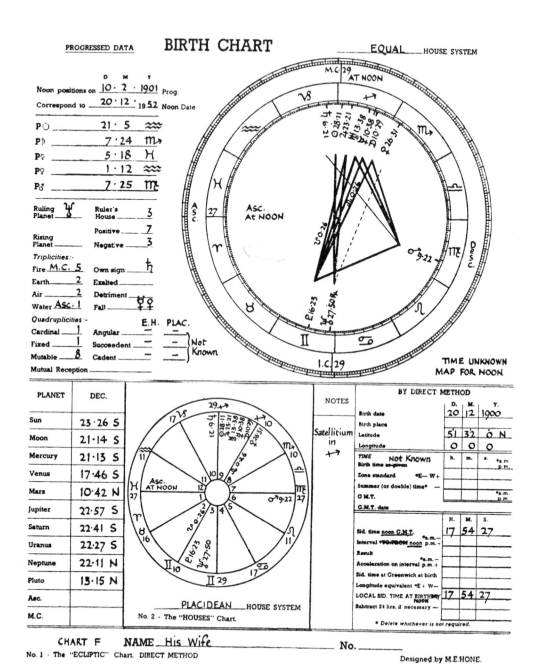

BIRTH CHART

PROGRESSED DATA   EQUAL ___ HOUSE SYSTEM

	D	M	Y	
Noon positions on	10 · 2 · 1901 Prog.

Correspond to ___ 20·12· 19 52 Noon Date

P☉	21 · 5	♒
P☽	7·24	♏
P☿	5·18	♓
P♀	1·12	♒
P♂	7·25	♏

Ruling Planet	♅	Ruler's House	3
Rising Planet		Positive	7
		Negative	3

Triplicities:-
Fire _M.C. 5_   Own sign _♄_
Earth __2__   Exalted ____
Air ___2___   Detriment ___
Water _Asc. 1_   Fall __☿♀__

Quadruplicities:-   E.H. PLAC.
Cardinal __1__   Angular ___ — —
Fixed ___1___   Succeedent _ — — } Not Known
Mutable __8__   Cadent ___ — —
Mutual Reception _____

M.C. 29 AT NOON
ASC. At NOON
I.C. 29
TIME UNKNOWN
MAP FOR NOON

PLANET	DEC.
Sun	23·26 S
Moon	21·14 S
Mercury	21·13 S
Venus	17·46 S
Mars	10·42 N
Jupiter	22·57 S
Saturn	22·41 S
Uranus	22·27 S
Neptune	22·11 N
Pluto	13·15 N
Asc.	
M.C.	

PLACIDEAN ___ HOUSE SYSTEM
No. 2 - The "HOUSES" Chart.

NOTES

Satellitium in ↗

BY DIRECT METHOD

	D.	M.	Y.
Birth date	20	12	1900
Birth place			
Latitude	51	32	0 N
Longitude	0	0	0

TIME _Not Known_   h. | m. | s. | °a.m. p.m.
Birth time as given
Zone standard   °E — W +
Summer (or double) time° —   °a.m. p.m.
G.M.T.
G.M.T. date

	H.	M.	S.
Sid. time noon G.M.T.	17	54	27

Interval TO/FROM noon p.m. +   °a.m. p.m. +
Result
Acceleration on interval p.m. +
Sid. time at Greenwich at birth
Longitude equivalent °E + W—

LOCAL SID. TIME AT BIRTHDAY NOON | 17 | 54 | 27
Subtract 24 hrs. if necessary —

* Delete whichever is not required.

CHART F   NAME _His Wife_ _____   No. _____
No. 1 - The "ECLIPTIC" Chart. DIRECT METHOD

Designed by M.E.HONE.

Extracts from Letters from Client to Astrologer

" Forces operating about me are *distracting*. When I thought of consulting an astrologer it seemed so silly to consult anyone else as to what one should do or not do. Moreover, I do not think that the responsibility for a decision should be put on another even though that other is capable. Nevertheless, I would like your observations so that I might understand the better ; so perhaps you could treat this as a sort of academic problem so that I might appreciate more fully the advantages of astrology.

" The present circumstances are almost identical to those which I experienced in 1939–40. I was then living with my first wife when someone else came along and caused great joy, but such was my belief in duty, that in spite of conditions being easy for me to go off with her, I did not do this, thus causing myself great suffering. Eventually my marriage did come to an end by which time I had lost track of that other. In any case I had made up my mind that I would be more careful next time and after my divorce was an unattached person for a period, but now (summer 1952) I have again met someone who brings back all the feelings of harmony I experienced before ; this time, I seem to have outgrown duty and the like and would go off to-morrow if I could, but conditions are not as easy as before ; what I mean is that I cannot now see that any good can come of a thing by shattering something or someone to achieve that end. I get quite involved in all kinds of philosophical arguments with myself, the differences between fate and destiny, desire and will and so on. However, as near as I can get to it, there is some kind of tension, repression or casualness from my wife to me, whereas from the other there is intensity and vitalness. I have always felt I wanted to do something, to fight for some cause, though what it is to be I scarcely know, but I feel there is more chance of it maturing when with ' the other.' But what about my wife ? What is the real relationship between myself and the two of them ? Is there some mistake *in me* that causes me to make these two mistakes or is it just a matter of getting evolved ?

" If only I could get this thing settled, I feel I could do good work in one sphere or another, or is this just an illusion ? I suppose my will-power is strong enough to stop it but then I would eliminate feeling and this in turn would eliminate incentive and so a deadlock would be reached ! Fundamentally, I believe that every personality should have the conditions which enable it to flower, expand and create ; this demands the removal of as much tyranny of any kind as is possible.

" When you do my analysis, please be *quite frank*, don't spare me."

EXAMINATION OF CHARTS OF THE MAN, HIS WIFE AND THE OTHER*
Significators†

He :—
Satellitium ♋

Wife :—
Satellitium ♐

The very first glance at the three charts tells almost the whole story.

You and your present wife are each in your way extremists. *You* have four planets in one sign Cancer with two more from the tail end of Gemini and one in the beginning of Leo turning this into a mass of seven of the ten planets collected within 44 degrees of the 360. That in itself constitutes a problem for the person who has it and for the person or persons who have to live with him !

* Notes and three fore-pages are omitted to save space.
† Significators entered on astrologer's carbon copy only.

For you, life can never be equable or ordinary. It must always go in leaps and bounds. I wish I were certain just how much astrology you know so that I could decide on the manner in which to explain this to you. I intensely dislike plastering an analysis with astrological terms which are not understandable to the reader, yet, if they *are* understood, I can make myself clear in a few lines instead of a few pages. So excuse me if I am talking in too elementary a fashion for what you do know or too advanced a way for what you *don't* know !

Can you see that if the usual variety in a human being is produced by the natures of the different planets working in different modes in the different signs, then there is a marked one-pointedness if several are working in one mode ? Further, if several are working in the sphere of life actively denoted by one house, this again constitutes a singleness of direction at any one time. Now add to that the constant passage of the planets by progression and transit and you will see that if one compulsive force activates the working of the principles of seven planets in quick succession, there *must* be upheavals in the life.

♂ ☌ ♅
☍ ☽ ♆ ☉
in ♋ in 6th

Now this is quite enough for one man but on to it is piled the most forceful, disruptive, harsh, energising, invigorating, crashing, galvanic conjunction possible. That is, Mars and Uranus together, closely in opposition to your Neptunised Sun and Moon in Cancer. Putting it into plain English, you are *deeply* sensitive, intuitional, impressionable, almost mediumistic. You are imbued with the most visionary ideas coming through your unconscious self from heaven alone knows where, since you are an open " disc " on which recordings are made tele-pathically, psychically, sympathetically. All this is *exaggeratedly* so because of the conjunction of Jupiter, and the whole thing, being in the 6th house, impels you to *do* something about it. *Of course* you long to " do " something for someone or some cause ! The essence of the 6th house is " service " in the widest meaning (look up in text-book). It isn't that some ideal has captured your mind ; it is that you just *want* to feel that all your capability for sound ordering and building up (Capricorn Ascendant) should be properly used in a protective way (Cancerian satellitium) for what might be called " mothering " or " nursing " something. You want to see something growing under your eyes ; something which *you* have nurtured. But with the pre-ponderance of receptivity in your nature, you need to have this *vitalised*, almost as a feminine plant needs to be fertilised. This carries no impli-cation of lack of masculinity in you but it means that your function is to receive intuitively and to build with the encouragement and shaping which someone else can give you.

☉ ☌ ♃ in 6th

7 negative planets
5 in Water,
1 only in Fire

Ruler in ♓

♄, ruler
□ ♀

Yet, what have you to reckon with ? This avalanche, this tornado from the hidden depths of you (12th house) always upsetting you and everyone with you.

Thus, your chart falls into these two main sections, with a third as a further difficulty, for the position of your ruler (Saturn) is such that harmony in life and easy relationships with others are *extremely* difficult, (square Venus).

♃ ☌ cusp 7

Naturally, such relationships will crowd on you ; you can't avoid them, but you can't handle them. It is hard to draw a parallel. I can only think of a man on skis rushing down the snowy slopes of a mountain, thrilled by every moment, side by side with another expert skier wildly enjoying everything, yet one false move or one hidden rock and both may crash in a moment.

It seems to me that you must always expect life to have violent contrasts of light and colour and you must enjoy them while they last but not expect them to be permanent. As soon as you try to cage them, they will be spoilt. You must enjoy what you can, but it is better to keep it as a bright gleam and not try to turn it into an oil lamp to light the kitchen.

Ψ ☍ ♅
intensified

Now I have only to hear that anyone is born in 1907 and I can tell them what their present trouble is without even opening an ephemeris. Look at your map and see the close opposition of Neptune and Uranus which recurred five times in a few years and lasted weeks each time, thus turning out hundreds of you with tense nervous systems, capable also of stresses to the last limit of endurance (and many have not endured). Add Mars to one end of this ; add Sun and Moon to the other and what a conflagration you have started !

♃ ☌ ☉ △ ♄

see-saw except for
♄

Fortunately, you have the expansion, that is the capacity for enjoyment and pulling things off which is gained from Jupiter being conjunct your Sun and trine your ruler, Saturn. These are virtually your only helpful contacts. Your whole life is a forceful attempt to level a balance which the slightest wind upsets.

♃ ☌ cusp 7

Given a chance, yours is the nature which does great things because it can visualise them but this humdrum world isn't very full of such chances. Moreover, your chances must come through *others*. In one of your letters, you expressed something of this sort which you instinctively know.

T ♅ ♋

Now why do I know so well that one after another of the 1907's will be coming along in distress ? It is because the slow transit of Uranus, seven years to cover thirty degrees, is now half-way through Cancer. But because of your *seven* planets within 44 degrees, it will take about 10½ years to finish upsetting you ! It has been at its worst in these last few years while it has been backwards and forwards over the tenth and twelfth degrees because it then has not been only over the degree occupied by Neptune at your birth but opposite those occupied by itself and Mars.

In my opinion (*not* advice !) the only way you can sooth this distracting situation is by *work*, by constructive work in which you form an organisation or a building which has come out of your own imagination and dreams. You were doing this during the years when you perfected that intricate invention about which you told me, although you may not have realised this. You put a dream of abstract ideas into concrete form and it gave you satisfaction.

This Uranian transit has to go over your Sun three times in the coming year—14th August, 13th January and 31st May. At no time are other transits helpful, and, when the third time comes, the extra assertiveness which you will get through a transit of Mars over those seven planets will be enough to disrupt everything.

Do you know the times taken for the different transits to recur ? Mars takes two years round the circle so it energises those seven planets from conjunction, two squares and opposition during that time. When there is so much pressure already at work, will you be surprised if the fireworks go off !

Now the point is, what are you going to *do* about it ? As I said, your chart shows the inflammability of the time. This is where some measure of freewill comes in. With your Capricorn Ascendant and its ruler Saturn in Pisces, you have a good sense of caution and can look ahead. You also have a gentleness which can include a kindly sympathy, in spite of all the tendency to disrupt. It seems hardly possible that you will go through the next two years without making definite changes. What matters is that you should *make* them, that is make them *yourself*, with planned deliberation, not have them forced on you so that you act hastily and without forethought. The three dates mentioned are likely to leave you upset and irritable, but later on, when the transit comes to Jupiter, you should then get more opportunity for fulfilment. After that, the transit will be on the cusp of your 7th house (partners) and it is not unlikely that a change will occur. Dates for transit to Jupiter : 3rd week August 1953, continuing for months close to 7th cusp ; middle fortnight of January 1954 ; first half of June 1954, coming to cusp 7 again in July.

With regard to the attraction you spoke of in 1939–40 it is interesting to note that Mercury, the only planet in the part of your chart which has to do with close associations, was so placed that any such thing would have been strongly accented at the time ; moreover, there was a doubled effect, since Venus, significator of bringing together in harmony, was activating Mercury, further urging you to just what you describe. Unfortunately, these two planets are so situated in your chart that the basic urges which they represent do not smoothly have their way.

⊙ p ⌐ ♆ p
♀ p ⚹ ♇
  ⊡ ♂ r
Asc. p △ ♂
  ♄ △ ♂ O-D
  ☽ ⚹ ♇ O-D
  ☽ p ⽊

For transits
see progressed
chart-form

♃ ♂ cusp 7

♅ rules 2nd

⊙ p enters ♍
♀ p ⊼ Asc.
  ☐ ♅ p

PRESENT TIME

A study of present progressions gives an idea of just what is the case ; it is best described as an inability to see your way in front of you (Sun p. semi-square Neptune p.). The time can be used for artistic or intuitional matters but otherwise it must be described as a time for care against any kind of deceit or illusion.

August
14th
As already remarked, disruptive and irritating.

24th
Depressing. Try to counter this by calm occupation which interests you.

September
29th
The end of the month is again frustrating and depressing. Let it pass.

October
Now (and again in early November and a third time in May) you get the added effect of the current Neptune–Saturn conjunction square the degree of your Jupiter. These cardinal squares which are forming this year are an uneasy business and there is much talk of them in astrological circles. Look after financial affairs at these times and use your natural caution over affairs with others ; *all* " others."

26th–29th
Now you are conscious of a keen desire to get started on a new line of thought and action. This may affect your home conditions. It is indeed a suitable time to start any new enterprise.

November
As above.

December
6th
A more favourable and happier time.

1953

From a long-term point of view, this is the start of a less hectic and more practical attitude on your part.

January
13th
This is the second " disruptive " day. You might try smashing some breakables or fusing all the lights in the house by way of working it off on things instead of people ! ! ! Even so, the " more favourable " and cheerfully energetic mood of last month continues. A very good time for intuitive and inventive ideas which can be constructive.

February
3rd

Not a good time for dealing with subordinates. Avoid trouble with them.

March and April

Work seems important, possible changes being made.

May
31st

Third " disruptive " day.

23rd–25th

As around 5th October and 6th November.

June and July

These two months should be full of incident. Your home, your work, and your ideas should be affected so that you are extremely busy, ending in a more successful time about 15th July.

⊙ p ⊻ ♃ p
♀ p ☌ ♄ p
☽ ♈
T's ♃ good

1954

In both spring and summer, there are happy times and opportunities for enjoyment. Your mood is active and forceful.

♂ p ☌ ♅ p
♀ p ☌ ♄ r
☽ ♈
T ♅ ☌ 7th
T ♃ ☌ ♃ △ ♄ ☌ ☿

1955

The general outlook seems much better because of changes made.

⊙ p □ M.C.
T ♄ ☌ M.C.
☿ p ⚹ ♇
T ♃ □ M.C. ⊼
Asc.
♀ p ⚹ ♀

1956

Business will take your attention closely. There is probably added responsibility. This year marks the end of the long Uranus transit over the seven planets.

COMPARISON WITH CHART OF SECOND WIFE

(Time unknown—chart set for noon.)

It is not difficult to see why you and your wife came together and why the " casualness " of which you speak, has grown up between you.

Like you, she is an extremist. Like you she has a group of planets massed in one part of her chart. She has six within twenty-four degrees and, in fact, seven within forty degrees. Like you, she has two planets opposing these and a solitary one, Mars, in square to three of them. As her birth time is not known, it is not possible to say which is emphasised as ruler. Nor can we know in which house this satellitium falls. All that can be said is that her self-expressiveness and outgoing side would be very attractive to you. You would have seen in her that *positivity* which you need as a spark to your own *receptivity*. But the strongly Sagittarian person does like a great amount of personal and mental freedom. It is quite extraordinary that you each have Jupiter

She :—
Satellitium in Fire
He :—
Satellitium in Water

BIRTH CHART

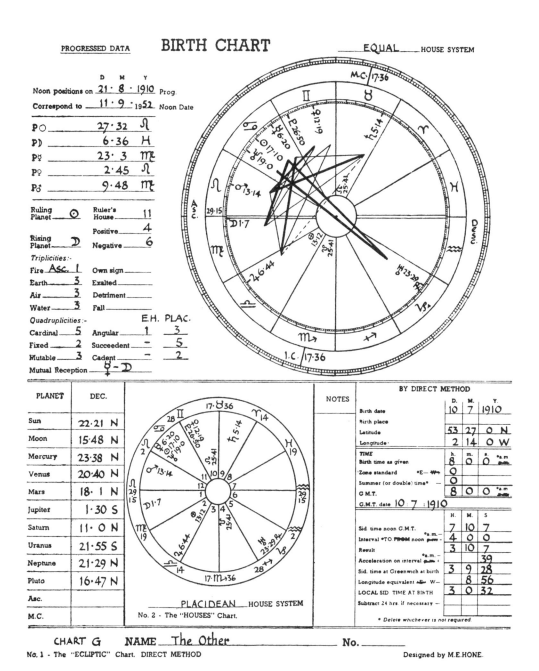

PROGRESSED DATA

EQUAL HOUSE SYSTEM

	D	M	Y	
Noon positions on	21	8	1910	Prog.
Correspond to	11	9	1952	Noon Date

P⊙	27·32	♌
P☽	6·36	♓
P☿	23·3	♍
P♀	2·45	♌
P♂	9·48	♍

Ruling Planet	⊙	Ruler's House	11
		Positive	4
Rising Planet	☽	Negative	6

Triplicities:-
Fire **Asc. 1** Own sign _____
Earth **3** Exalted _____
Air **3** Detriment _____
Water **3** Fall _____

Quadruplicities:-
		E.H.	PLAC.
Cardinal	5	Angular 1	3
Fixed	2	Succeedent —	5
Mutable	3	Cadent —	2
Mutual Reception	☿ – ☽		

PLANET	DEC.
Sun	22·21 N
Moon	15·48 N
Mercury	23·38 N
Venus	20·40 N
Mars	18· 1 N
Jupiter	1·30 S
Saturn	11· 0 N
Uranus	21·55 S
Neptune	21·29 N
Pluto	16·47 N
Asc.	
M.C.	

NOTES

PLACIDEAN HOUSE SYSTEM
No. 2 - The "HOUSES" Chart.

BY DIRECT METHOD

	D.	M.	Y.
Birth date	10	7	1910
Birth place			
Latitude	53	27	0 N
Longitude	2	14	0 W

	h.	m.	s.
TIME Birth time as given	8	0	0 *a.m.—
Zone standard *E— W—	0		
Summer (or double) time*	0		
G.M.T.	8	0	0 *a.m.

G.M.T. date 10·7·1910

	H.	M.	S.
Sid time noon G.M.T.	7	10	7 *a.m.—
Interval *TO FROM noon p.m.—	4	0	0
Result	3	10	7
Acceleration on interval *a.m.— +			39
Sid. time at Greenwich at birth	3	9	28
Longitude equivalent *E— W—		8	56
LOCAL SID TIME AT BIRTH	3	0	32
Subtract 24 hrs. if necessary —			

*Delete whichever is not required.

CHART G NAME **The Other** No. _____

No. 1 - The "ECLIPTIC" Chart. DIRECT METHOD

Designed by M.E.HONE.

COMPARISON TABLE

HIS WIFE | **"THE OTHER WOMAN"**

HIS WIFE

The Man	☉	☽	☿	♀	♂	♃	♄	♅	♆	♇
☉					*1°					
☽										
☿		△3°	△3°							
♀	☍				△3°					
♂				△1°						
♃					△1° *3°					
♄	□1°					☍ exact			□ exact	
♅										
♆										
♇										
Asc.										
M.C.										

SUMMARY

Exact aspects	3
Within 1° of orb.	5
Within 3° of orb.	4
Harmonious aspects	8
Inharmonious aspects	4

"THE OTHER WOMAN"

The Man	☉	☽	☿	♀	♂	♃	♄	♅	♆	♇	Asc.	MC
☉	☌1°								☌3°			
☽			☌2°			□2°	*3°					
☿						*1°	□2°					
♀												
♂												
♃							☍2°	☌2°				
♄									☌2°	□1°		
♅												
♆												
♇								☌1°				
Asc.		□2°										
M.C.												

SUMMARY

Exact aspects	—
Within 1° of orb.	4
Within 2° of orb.	7
Within 3° of orb.	2
Harmonious	8
Inharmonious	5

conjunct the Sun, and in each case five degrees away, and each has the
Moon in the same sign as the Sun. With this decidedness of pattern in
each of you, it must be a marriage of opposites. *You* have a need to
take care of someone but *she* needs independence. She is quicker and
more brisk than you (remember this is without the modification
of knowledge of her Ascending degree). The Water part of you is apt
to feel heated and upset by the Fire part of her, while the Earth part of
you can feel scorched by her Fire. On her part, she would feel that your
Earth and Water are putting out the Fire of her enthusiasm and independence. To you, at present, this independence seems a casualness
and a lack of *rapport* with you. There should be mental reciprocity
since your Mercury, like hers, expresses itself through a sign of the fire
triplicity.

As you say, " every personality should have the conditions which
enable it to flower, expand and create." She needs a wider freedom
than marriage permits nowadays. She should have plenty of exercise
and out-of-door life of a vigorous kind, and considerable width of
reading and time to study. Most women get neither of these freedoms
now. She is somewhat hot-headed and also has a certain escapist
tendency and would like freedom but it is late in life for her to start
being free now, unless she can fill life with her own interests. Unless the
unknown Ascendant would give a different emphasis, it does not seem
that she is very personally affectionate. She can be strenuous over
anything she sets her hand to but can exhaust herself, tiring her nerves.

COMPARISON WITH CHART OF " THE OTHER "

Now whereas yours and your wife's chart were extraordinarily
alike in their same shaping but strong difference of *mode* of expression,
this chart is completely otherwise, in that the shaping is quite different
but the *mode* of expression is more similar.

Born in 1910, your friend has the later opposition of Uranus and
Neptune, and, like you, she has a close conjunction of Sun with this
Neptune, also Mercury in Cancer. *She therefore understands your
receptivity because she has it herself.*

She has considerable strength of character and purpose and also
a " way with her " of getting what she wants easily and of sensibly
planning her life. She has a practical ability in dealing with affairs
but her main link with you is that lively desire to " look after " and
" nurse " which most Cancerians have. She has the same inspirational,
idealistic feelings as yourself and would respond to your personal care-
fulness of her since she would like to be looked after and would not feel
this as any curtailment of her freedom. Yet, at the same time, her
courage and strength of character is such (Mars in Leo) that she has
that spark which, as you say, vitalises you.

The birth time given is 8 a.m. but this was probably approximate.
It gives 29° 15′ Leo as Ascendant so one hesitates to make definite

☉ ☍ ♅
♂ in ♌
☉ ☿ ♋
♃ in ♎
☽ in ♍

statements as to her Ascending sign being Leo or Virgo. She must seem strongly Leo since her Sun has been progressing through that sign for the last twenty-eight years. Her Moon has recently entered her 7th house, so she would be propulsively inclined towards a close relationship in life. She has a freer expression of self than either you or your wife. She has a very definite and determined personality and would not want to play second fiddle, yet she has a home-making sense and a genius for companionship, a lovable nature and plenty of common sense.

PRESENT TIME

As her birthday is so close to yours, it is obvious that she must have those three " disruptive " days like you. Uranus moves so slowly that the times will be much the same, exactitude being 29th August, 22nd December, 14th June. The tiresome Saturn–Neptune upsets her also, both in the last months of 1952 and in the spring of 1953.

☉ p ∟ ♃
but T's of ♃
difficult

She seems to wish for expansion in life this year, but not to have too much opportunity, but her mind seems very alive and ready for changes. She has had the same galvanic but upsetting time as yourself during the early days of the passage of Uranus through Cancer (on her Mercury and your Moon), and now will share its transit on the Suns of both of you and then over her Neptune and opposition to her Uranus. This will be nervously tense for her. Both will feel like making a break. *This must be a matter of decision not rash action.*

☿ p △ ♅
6 aspects by O-D

She has some good aspects in the years ahead ; for definite action in 1954 and for a new phase to begin in 1956.

☉ p ☌ Asc.
♃ p ⚹ ♂
♀ p □ ♄
☽ enters ♈

☉ p ☌ ☽
♂ p □ ♀

There are many close contacts between the two charts, the main ones being those between the Cancerian planets, you with your Jupiter bringing a fuller vision of life to her intuitional and, can we say " mystical " understanding, while she with her Mercury brings a mental stimulus to your receptive Moon.

We seem to finish where we began ; that this is an academic study, not a piece of advice. It has been most interesting work for me. Let us hope it interests you too !

Extracts from Client's Letters Commenting on Analysis

" Many thanks for your analysis ; all I need now is a strait-jacket and a box of sleeping pills so as to be ready for the disruptive days ! I would like to deal with the analysis objectively as it is quite remarkable how right many of your remarks are ; I do not want you to misunderstand me when I say that only up to a point am I interested in myself while beyond that, I am interested in understanding the truth in things, though this may always be only comparative and never absolute.

" I think the analysis is very practical and I like the way it is put together. I wish I had had it when I was younger. It is only in the last few years that I have realised that I assess a person's make-up through the feeling he or she *induces in me*, and if I had known that earlier it would have been of practical benefit. Therefore your comments about preponderance of receptivity are interesting. How much I agree that it requires to be vitalised by someone else! I have often felt like a good violin waiting to be played upon. But there are other aspects of this and I wonder whether they show in the chart ? That is, this vitalisation can only take place first if there is sympathy, then there must be truthfulness and wholesomeness, then a respect and admiration which has to pass a critical screen ; and finally there has to be a reason *why* I should allow myself to be vitalised : but the memories of John Knox are dimming so the reason is now not so difficult to find, so let us say it is the pursuit of happiness !

" Then about work. Only when I'm putting into it everything I've got can I be happy so that I feel justified at the end of the day.

" As to the personal relationship, I have such a strong feeling of being able to *do* something when working with ' the other.' Would it always be satisfying ? or would it become, as you said, like the oil lamp in the kitchen ? But an oil lamp has a mellow glow and is soothing !

" Sometimes I think I have too great a degree of caution which causes inaction so that, as you say, I need shaping from someone else, yet a shaping with which I would never be in conflict. Then, almost at once, I see the world as the honing-stone and the individual as the knife being sharpened and tempered to become finer and purer. But why ? For what ? For when ? If I were writing a treatise I would call it ' The Doctrine of the *Inevitability* of Perfection.'

" Astrology captures my imagination. It seems to get to the essence of things."

Later extracts (see note on October 26–29th)

" After your long academic analysis I could see I had to take some action. I saw I ought to have a ' baby '—and, amazingly, I had an original idea and have already patented it and started a company to make it ; so, for the present, I'll look after this ' child ' which, I think, was born from the union with ' the Other.' "

BIRTH CHART

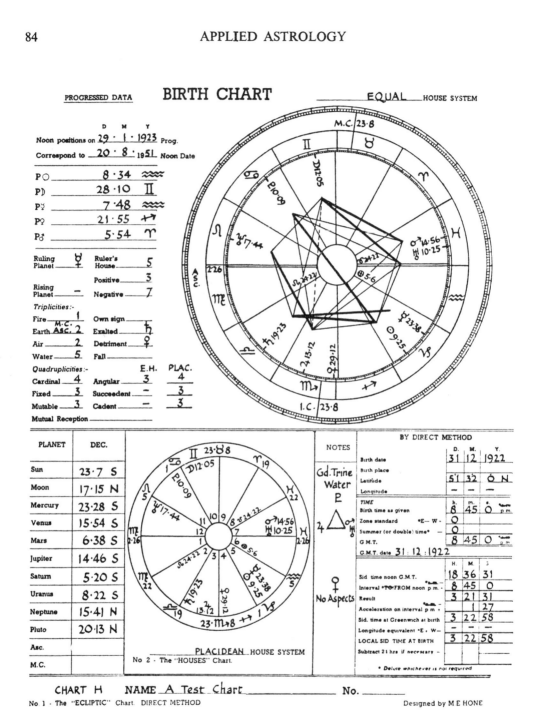

PROGRESSED DATA   **BIRTH CHART**   EQUAL HOUSE SYSTEM

Noon positions on 29 · 1 · 1923 Prog.

Correspond to 20 · 8 · 1951 Noon Date

P☉	8·34	♒
P☽	28·10	♊
P☿	7·48	♒
P♀	21·55	♐
P♂	5·54	♈

Ruling Planet	☿	Ruler's House 5
		Positive 3
Rising Planet	—	Negative 7

Triplicities:-

Fire	M.C. 1	Own sign —
Earth	Asc. 2	Exalted ♄
Air	2	Detriment ♀
Water	5	Fall —

Quadruplicities:-

		E.H.	PLAC.
Cardinal	4	Angular 3	4
Fixed	3	Succeedent —	3
Mutable	3	Cadent —	3

Mutual Reception _____

M.C. 23·8
I.C. 23·8

PLANET	DEC.
Sun	23·7 S
Moon	17·15 N
Mercury	23·28 S
Venus	15·54 S
Mars	6·38 S
Jupiter	14·46 S
Saturn	5·20 S
Uranus	8·22 S
Neptune	15·41 N
Pluto	20·13 N
Asc.	
M.C.	

PLACIDEAN HOUSE SYSTEM
No 2 - The "HOUSES" Chart.

NOTES

Gd. Trine
Water
P
♃ △ ♂

♀
No Aspects

BY DIRECT METHOD

	D.	M.	Y.
Birth date	31	12	1922
Birth place			
Latitude	51	32	0 N
Longitude	—	—	—

	h.	m.	s.
TIME Birth time as given	8	45	0 p.m.
Zone standard *E – W –	0		
Summer (or double) time*	—		
G.M.T.	8	45	0 p.m.

G.M.T. date 31 · 12 : 1922

	H.	M.	S.
Sid. time noon G.M.T.	18	36	31
Interval *TO FROM noon p.m.	8	45	0
Result	3	21	31
Acceleration on interval p.m. +		1	27
Sid. time at Greenwich at birth	3	22	58
Longitude equivalent *E · W —	—	—	—
LOCAL SID TIME AT BIRTH	3	22	58
Subtract 24 hrs if necessary –			

* Delete whichever is not required

No 1 - The "ECLIPTIC" Chart. DIRECT METHOD

CHART H   NAME A Test Chart   No. _____

Designed by M E HONE

CHAPTER 11

" BLIND " ASTROLOGY

Chart H—A Test Chart

Reasons for Inclusion

It is the writer's definite conviction that *applied astrology* in the meaning of astrological technique used to help people in time of need, should be *consultative*. The client should supply a case history, as to doctor or psychologist, and the trouble should then be discussed in the light of the client's personal knowledge and the astrologer's deductions from the chart.

However, there are times when it may be agreed to withhold all case-history in order that a serious investigator may find out exactly what can be done by astrological technique alone.

In this spirit, an editor asked one of his writers on special subjects to make such an investigation. Here is his published statement* :—

Editor's Statement

" I asked the writer of this article to obtain a test horoscope of someone whose life and exact birth moment were known to her. The subject chosen was a young married woman who was totally unknown to the astrologer. Here are her comments on the horoscope and reading (which were prepared by Mrs. Margaret E. Hone). Readers must judge for themselves whether the information is sufficient.—Editor."

Method of Working

Notes were made similar to those prefacing Chart A, but not with such detail since the accustomed worker does not need this. The journalist came and took down in shorthand exactly what the practitioner said speaking from these notes. The only conversation which took place before this was that the journalist was asked whether she would prefer not to hear any comments on the marriage of the girl in question as it was considered not to be a satisfactory one. Her reply was that she wished to hear whatever was thought to be true.

Journalist's Report to Editor after Interview

The journalist's report to her editor was as follows :—

" I know intimately the young woman who is the subject of this horoscope, and although, of course, I cannot express an opinion on the notes as to future influences, the character delineation seems to me remarkably full and true. The entire extent of the information supplied was (a) moment, date and place of birth ; (b) that she was married.

" On the basis of this it was correctly deduced that she had had connection with the sea in the war (actually she was a naval V.A.D.), that she had married an airman and that the marriage was drawing to a close.

" I cannot detect a single false conclusion, and the description of influences and tendencies for the future must be of the greatest value to her."

*Quoted by kind permission of the Editor of *Answers*, 31st March, 1951.

Written Analysis

At the journalist's request, the chart and written analysis were prepared so that the girl might have them. As usual, the prologue and page of notes were supplied and further comments were then made.

Journalist's Report to Editor after full Analysis Given

The reading supplied would fill several pages of *Answers* ; it consists of

(*a*)   A Prologue, setting forth what astrology undertakes to do and for what purpose.

(*b*)   Notes on the chart, or horoscope, explaining the method by which it is interpreted and drawing attention to salient features.

(*c*)   A Personal Analysis. This sets out in great detail the subject's qualities, characteristics and idiosyncracies, mental powers and attitudes, spare-time occupations ; governing conditions in her friendships, love, and marriage ; difficulties likely to arise ; dangers inherent in her particular combination of qualities ; her probable rôle in the 1939–45 war ; a great change at the age of 20 (" which was undoubtedly marriage and change of personal circumstance "). Husband would be in the Navy or Air Force. A likelihood of the marriage being ended within two years ; the effect of this unfortunate marriage on the subject's character ; advice on re-orientation in this respect. Aptitude for secretarial work and for writing. Children (" with your love of children you will undoubtedly have one child or more." Actually she has one).

(*d*)   An indication of the probabilities for the present time (with a hint of major changes in 1952 and 1957) : for 1951, month by month, indicating the vital periods in each ; and for every year up to and including 1960."

Astrologer's first impressions from the Chart

1.   Ascendant, M.C., Sun and Mercury in Earth imply solidity and caution personally.

2.   Mars conjunction Uranus in Water in 7th imply just the reverse in dealing with others in close connection.

3.   The squares from these to Moon in 10th imply that the career will be set back through their action in the life.

4.   The trines from these to Jupiter in 3rd imply an expansion of mind through them also.

5.   The semi-sextile of the Sun to Uranus in 7th (to which it is sextile at birth) in 1953 implies freedom from marriage by then.

PERSONAL ANALYSIS*

Significators†

Asc., M.C., Sun and ruler of Asc. all in Earth— ♍, ♑ yet ♂ ☌ ♅ in ♓ ☐ ☽ in 10th at mid-point of these two in 7th

To try to condense a long description, one might say you are a *prudent individualist*, vitally going out for life and experience, having a good brain and good basic forethought and ambition ; having a curious mixture within you of virginal restraint and yet vivid keenness for life, trying to combine a cool attitude with a sentimental outrush, thus making your own life difficult and your career spoilt through lack of ability to integrate these two sides of your nature in your dealings with others.

* Notes and three fore-pages omitted to save space.
† Significators entered on astrologer's carbon copy only.

♑
♄ in 2nd

♍

♓ on 7th

♑
♍

☿ in ♑ △ M.C.
(exact)
♃ in ♏ in 3rd
♃ △ ♅

♏

☉ and Asc.-ruler
in 5th

☉ in 5th in ♑

Asc. ♍

☉ and Asc.-ruler
in 5th
☉ ✶ ♅ and ♂
in 7th

☉ in 5th
strongly asp.

☿ △ M.C.
♃ in 3rd

♂, ♅ in 7th
☐ ☽ in 10th
♆, rules 7th
☐ M.C.

as above, also ♀
unaspected

7th

♓ on 7th

♂ in 7th

To go into detail on these points : you are essentially practical, sensible, calm, prudent, able, far-sighted, wishing to make detailed plans to secure your own interests, especially financially. You have a love for detail, an analytical appreciation of whatever job lies to your hand, a strong desire to be helpful to others even if this means sacrifice to yourself. You can plan, wait, prepare, organise and manage. You have charm in a dainty provocative way.

MENTALLY, you are excellently equipped. You have the ability to profit by advanced tuition and training in your chosen line and this should have been to do with hygiene or health and through science to this end. You have a distinct aptitude for *penetrative* thought, hence, once taught and having gained experience, you should be able to pursue research work with success.

In all your SPARE-TIME ACTIVITIES, you have an urge to express a great love for all creative activity. Needless to say, this must be expressed in different ways, at different stages in your life.

As a child, you would have thrown yourself into all games, amusements, acting, and anything which meant a building up or constructing. In this you would enjoy tackling a detailed task with small parts to assemble. You would express yourself in art in a quiet way. Then you would be vitally interested in your love affairs, but stimulating to others, rather than being over-stirred yourself.

After this, being a woman, you would express your creativity in love of children and desire to bring them up with all care. *But*, it is highly important that, at your present age, you do not think of this as all there is to do in life. You are too mentally constructive to let this swamp you and you must plan for the future when you can further develop yourself.

IN FRIENDSHIP, LOVE AND MARRIAGE, there is much to say, since the crux of your life and your happiness lies in the necessity of your understanding of yourself in your personal relationship with others, as soon as that relationship becomes a close one.

Here is the difficulty within you and the chief lack of integration in yourself. You must try to reason this out and plan for the future in the light of better knowledge of yourself.

From more than one indication, it is obvious that you find it hard to understand yourself when reciprocity and harmony are necessary. Perhaps the best way to explain is to say that your calm poise deserts you when brought into close and intimate relationships. Your thoroughly good desire to be kind and helpful to another, especially if that other calls out any pity or sympathy or need for care from you, leads you to a *sentimental* feeling which you mistake for depth of affection and you are inclined to rush into an inescapable tie-up. You then incline to stimulate your partner (whether this is a husband or a

♍
♂ ♅ □ ☽

Asc. ♍
Gd △ Water
♅ ruler 6th
♂ ♂ in ♓

☉ p ✶ ♀
☽ p ♂ 7th

♅ in ♓, 7th

♂ ♅ in 7th
□ ☽
☉ p to ⊻ ♅ 1953

♓ on 7th

♂ ♅ △ ♃ in 3rd

♑

♂ in 7th
♈ on 8th
♑ ♍

♓ 7th

☿, ruler, □ ♄

♃ in 3rd

♓ on 7th

♏ on 3rd
♃ △ ♅

♂, ♅ 7th

Asc. ♍
☽, ♊

☉ and ruler
in 5th

business or professional partnership) and to agitate too much about detail and to be overcome with too much repercussion on yourself, with drastic consequences liable to end in disruption.

It is part of your experience of life that you were a grown girl in the war years and therefore it seems likely that your mental and educational development was not fulfilled. It would appear that your war service was to do with the sea, so you were probably a Wren.

A great change took place at the age of 20 and this was undoubtedly marriage and change of personal circumstances. You would have met your husband through your career which would then have been in one of the services. He would also have been in the Navy or Air Force (perhaps the combination of Fleet Air Arm, but not Army).

It is impossible to feel that this can have been a success, and, in fact, it does seem as if this tie may be ended within the next two years. Your husband seems to have brought confusion into your life and to be somewhat incapable of clear-sighted action himself. The result must have been harsh on both of you.

No experience is valueless and this is shown to have had a tremendous affect on your *mind*. You may have suffered, but you have also grown mentally and you have a grasp of life and its sheer hard responsibilities such as you could not have had before. The point is— what are you going to make of this ? Your difficulty is that your desire to take a risk, to enjoy love and life is at variance with your real basic cautious, critical balanced self.

At all costs, you should try to realise that this *is* your real self, and that to lose this real self in a muddled sentimentality for someone else will *always* be as a trap for you, an entanglement which you must most warily avoid even if you are thereby more lonely at times.

As regards your CAREER, it follows on from what has been said, that your fine mental development cannot carry you through to the final objectives which you will set for yourself, if you allow yourself to be beset by people who confuse you and seek to work on your sympathy for their own advancement rather than your own.

You have an intuitive mind, capable of good training. It can be used in ways to do with medicine and science. You can be orderly and constructive and helpful if you throw in your lot with any people who are of the type who can help you in these ways. Even so, you must avoid *rushing* into any such partnership and must leave yourself loopholes for freedom both personally and mentally.

You could be the perfect secretary, but even now you should begin to develop your aptitude for writing.

With your love of children, you will undoubtedly have one child or more. Actual childbirth as an *event* is sometimes shown astrologically but as a natural recurrent happening in a woman's life, it

ħ rules 5th
ħ △ ☽

ħ △ ☽ 10th

♑
♂ ♅ 7th
Strong ħ
dispositor
☿, ruler, △ M.C.
exact

♂ ♅ 7th
☉ ☿ ♑

♂ ♅ △ ♃
♍

ħ in 2nd
strongly asp.
ħ, in 2nd in ♎
♆, ruler 7th, in 12th
⚹ ħ ⚹ ☽

☉ ♃
mainly benasp
♒ on 6th
♅ ☌ ♂
♀ unaspected

☿ □ ħ
ħ in 2nd

Asc. p. △ M.C.
△ ☿
☉ p ☌ ☿ p
in ♒ in 6th

M.C. p △ ħ
T ♇ ☌ ♆,
ruler 7th
see 1952

need not be strongly marked in a chart. What *is* marked, is the desire for children, the love of them and the ability to have them.

After this period in your life is over, there is much development ahead in public work for which you will fit yourself. Your success in this depends *vitally* on your understanding that you are, as first said, a prudent individualist, and that *firstly* mistaken sentiment, and *secondly* over-sudden assertiveness and dramatic action in relations with others, must be guarded against all through life. Enjoy your contacts, have a happy time, but learn to stand alone and to guard your own interests. This advice cannot be too much stressed in the endeavour to help you to make a success of your life.

You probably have no idea of your own dynamic effect on others. You know that you cannot live without the help and security which others can bring. Security is *necessary* to you, for without it you can have no peace of mind, so you must fully realise that those " others " whom you take to yourself in any form of " partnership " must be chosen by the exercise of your best self and all its careful ability to scrutinise. To criticise and fuss about detail in a possessive manner *after* you have chosen is to do it too late.

As to FINANCE, your progress is by slow building up rather than by speculation or the taking of risks. Also, your older years should be more full of stability than your present or your middle age. You will always have financial responsibilities and feel these keenly, but you will shoulder them bravely and others will help you, often behind the scenes.

Your HEALTH should not be a major worry as you have good robust vitality, good liver and good digestion. The weaknesses shown are firstly in the circulatory system, this being apparent in that you tend to suffer from cold feet and should therefore take plenty of exercise and wear warm boots in winter. Be kind to yourself in this respect. Later in life, you will need to look after your kidneys and you must, even now, realise that you have a nervous system and that worry, particularly financial worry, can overtax it and spoil your happiness. With your sane outlook, you will readily realise that attention to detail and wise planning will save much fussing and worrying.

PRESENT TIME

The whole essence of the present time is the emphasis on new beginnings and a new outlook on life. Your mental outlook is changing and you are more ready to take a detached view of life and to think of yourself as a worker in an interesting field. Many indications point to this main conclusion. You will not be able to put your plans into working order with all thoroughness until 1952. The intervening period is rather one of getting rid of present entanglements and preparation for an entirely new phase.

see 1957

The next period of *major* activity is in 1957, when again your own dynamism will stir others to action and you will again form a new close relationship with someone else. This *could* be a partnership for working purposes, but it is far more likely to be remarriage.

1951

☿ p ☌ ☉ p
    ∟ ♀ p

In this particular year, mental readjustment and unavoidable delay are in evidence. Activity is alert and restless. Attention is on the career and the safeguarding of yourself and family.

January

☽ p △ ♄ p
T ♆ ☌ ♄ in 2nd

♆ transit ends

This month has brought a certain amount of basic settlement which is very welcome. Unfortunately, financial worry is emphasised and your way seems anything but clear and will be so until late in March. The latter part of the month is the best.

24th–28th

T ♃ ✳ ☉
   △ ♇
   ☌ ♅

Around these days there should be more happiness, more change ending with an opportunity to make some change in an old relationship or to form a new one. Watch for this chance, since it should be advantageous.

February
5th–10th

T ♂ ☌ ♅ in 7th
   ☌ ♂ in 7th

A period of hectic activity with others and their affairs. All very exciting and also beneficial. As regards your health, there is a danger of accident through careless haste. Even so, it is a splendid time to start a working agreement with someone of the nature hinted at as it is to do with science or medicine. The word " science " must be taken to include all modern use of rays, waves, hence radio, wireless, television and so on.

10th–16th

T ♃ △ ♃ ☌ ♂

Strongly emphasised as time for assertive grasping of good opportunities and making the very best of them.

March

The month is more calm, though it cannot be said that you are settled in any way.

18th

T ♄ ✳ ♀

A minor happiness.

April and May

T ♇ direct
☌ ♆ in 12th

This is the strongest part of a six-month period of under-surface activity with regard to relations with others. Either you are quietly arranging a break or this is making itself concrete in your unspoken thoughts.

17th–18th (April)

T ♃ △ ♀

Good time to arrange a party or happy visit.

June

8th

T ♂ ♂ ☽ in 10th
T ♃ □ ☉ ♇

Definite urge to make changes in occupation. Great need to watch your step in your reactions to others and your effect on them.

27th

T ♅ ☍ ☉

Unexpected news or change affecting yourself. This could be through a child.

July

9th

T ♅ ♂ ♇

A dynamic day of action in regard to a friend. This is likely to be as a result of some disclosure.

14th

T ♅ △ ♅ r

Beneficial alteration of affairs likely and possible start of holiday.

August

5th

T ♄ ✶ ♀

Quietly happy.

T ☿ and ♀
both direct
T ♅ △ ♃

September

There is a distinct move forward in your affairs and there may be general improvement in health and outlook. More freedom of action.

October

9th

T ♂ ♂ Asc.

A day to use caution and go slowly.

T ♆ again
♂ ♄ in 2nd

16th

From now till the end of the year, the financial anxiety recurs.

T ♄ □ ☉ ♇
T ♄ △ ☽

November

1st–7th

A little depressing and frustrating, but better after 26th.

December

29th

T ♂ ♂ ♄

Minor irritations which should not be unduly stressed.

1952

☿ p ✶ ♂ p
Asc. p. △ M.C.
T ♆ ♂ ♄
T ♃ ☍ ♄ △ ♆
T ♄ ♂ ♄ r

A year of energetic mental application, with probability of starting a training for work. There are tiresome delays and unexpected changes and in the autumn comes a period of depression, but it is the real beginning of a new phase in life.

1953

☉ p ⊻ ♅ in 7th
(natal ✶)
♀ p ⊻ ☿
☽ p ☊
T ♃ ♂ M.C.

You should have achieved personal freedom by now and should find yourself much more able and managing and very glad to be free. In April–May, you should be able to improve your conditions considerably by more interesting work.

1954

☽ p in 12th
but in ♌
☉ p ⊻ ♅ p
T ♃ ☌ M.C.

It is likely that your occupation is now more behind the scenes, but with more authority in your hands. Changes are by no means over. These will be occasioned by friends and amongst friends. Occupation and money earning should be on the up grade with interesting developments in July.

1955

☉ p (natal 5th)
△ ☽ in 10th
T ♃ △ ♀

This should be a good year both for yourself, child or children, and for your prestige and position. Friends should be most helpful. September is a time of opportunity for happiness with someone very congenial.

1956

☉ p □ ♃ in 3rd
⊼ Asc.
☽ p ☌ Asc.
♂ p □ ☉

Difficulties occur, annoyances with daily companions, a move is possible and there is a general urge to action which should be carefully considered as *next year* is the better year for decisions.

1957

☉ p ⊻ ♂
    in 7th
♂ p ⊻ ♅
    in 7th

This is a most important year as rearrangements will be made and possible remarriage is extremely likely, though " partnership " as such may be for working reasons. In the autumn, the happy results of this should be obvious, with financial benefit.

1958

☉ p P ♃
☽ p ♎

Generally more peaceful and happy.

1959

♂ p ✳ ☽
in 10th

An accentuation on position and social affairs. With care as advised, in regard to all close relationships, this period can be most constructive.

1960

☉ p ☍ ♆
☽ p ♏ in 3rd

The attention turns to more abstract matters. With your essentially practical outlook, it would seem that you would now be able to give shape and form to abstract and intuitive ideas either in writing or painting. It is an expansive, mentally active period.

Do not forget that astrology is the interpretation of a symbolism and that this must be applied to affairs as they are at any one time. Also that, in the Prologue to this analysis, it was distinctly stated that the discussion was of *potentialities* for development and that the phrase " the likelihood is that " should precede all remarks as to future unfolding of the life pattern. Personal consultation is therefore preferable to work by post and I hope we shall meet at some time in the future.

Comment from Journalist at Time of Writing this Book in 1952

" As I told you in 1951, the girl whose chart you did was sure that she would be free from her unsatisfactory marriage before the end of that year, but astrological calculation seems to be correct for it is now 1952 and she has not yet got her divorce. Circumstances have been such that she could not set the ball rolling when she wanted to, but it is now likely that, as her chart showed, she will be free by 1953."

Final Comment from Journalist at Time of Going to Press, 1953

" I thought you would be interested to hear that your dating was correct. The girl completed her divorce early this year."

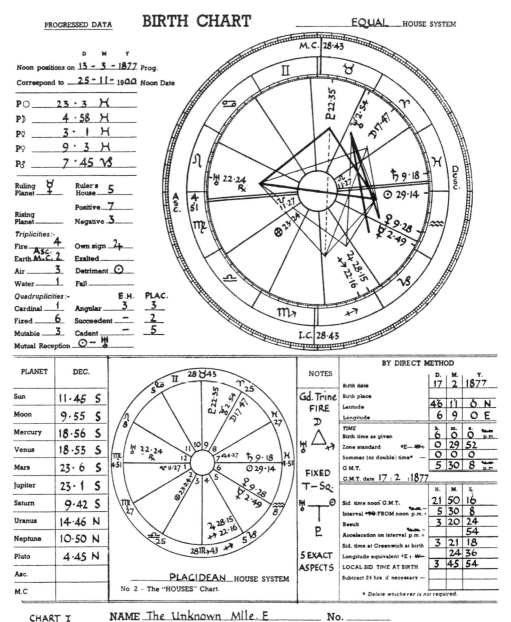

BIRTH CHART

PROGRESSED DATA   **BIRTH CHART**   EQUAL HOUSE SYSTEM

Noon positions on 13 - 3 - 1877 Prog.

Correspond to 25 - 11 - 1900 Noon Date

P⊙	23 · 3	♓
P☽	4 · 58	♓
P☿	3 · 1	♓
P♀	9 · 3	♓
P♂	7 · 45	♑

Ruling Planet ☿   Ruler's House 5

         Positive 7

Rising Planet   Negative 3

Triplicities:-
Fire 4   Own sign ♃
Earth 2   Exalted
Air 3   Detriment ⊙
Water 1   Fall

Asc. / M.C.

Quadruplicities:-

	E.H.	PLAC.
Cardinal 1 Angular	3	3
Fixed 6 Succeedent	—	2
Mutable 3 Cadent	—	5

Mutual Reception ⊙ — ♅

M.C. 28·43

I.C. 28·43

PLANET	DEC.
Sun	11·45 S
Moon	9·55 S
Mercury	18·56 S
Venus	18·53 S
Mars	23·6 S
Jupiter	23·1 S
Saturn	9·42 S
Uranus	14·46 N
Neptune	10·50 N
Pluto	4·45 N
Asc.	
M.C	

PLACIDEAN HOUSE SYSTEM

No 2 - The "HOUSES" Chart.

NOTES

Gd. Trine FIRE
☽ △ ♅

FIXED T-Sq.

♅ — ⊙ — ♇

5 EXACT ASPECTS

BY DIRECT METHOD

	D.	M.	Y.
Birth date	17	2	1877
Birth place			
Latitude	46	11	0 N
Longitude	6	9	0 E

	h.	m.	s.
TIME Birth time as given	6	0	0 p.m.
Zone standard *E— W+	0	29	52
Summer (or double) time*	0	0	0
G.M.T.	5	30	8 a.m.

G.M.T. date 17 : 2 : 1877

	H.	M.	S.
Sid. time noon G.M.T.	21	50	16
Interval +TO/FROM noon p.m.+	5	30	8
Result	3	20	24
Acceleration on interval p.m.+			54
Sid. time at Greenwich at birth	3	21	18
Longitude equivalent *E + W—		24	36
LOCAL SID TIME AT BIRTH	3	45	54
Subtract 24 hrs. if necessary —			

* Delete whichever is not required.

CHART I   NAME The Unknown Mlle. E   No. _____

No 1 - The "ECLIPTIC" Chart. DIRECT METHOD   Designed by M.E.HONE.

CHAPTER 12

" FORWARDS " ASTROLOGY, CONFIRMED BY " BACKWARDS " ASTROLOGY

Chart I.—The Unknown " Mademoiselle E "

Reasons for Inclusion

This chart is included because, as in Chart H, the work was done for publication and with the minimum of case-history. Its purpose in this book is to show that an astrologer trained in the deductive methods of forwards astrology, can apply his technique with speed, mentally synthesising outstanding factors, thus making a vignette of the person whose character he is deducing from the life-pattern of the birth-moment.

Case History

From an unknown correspondent, a letter arrived from Switzerland, saying that the writer, Lesley Blanch, was interested in the life of someone whom she would call " Mlle. E," and that she was about to publish a short biography of her and felt it would add to the interest if an astrological chart could be added with *very* short interpretation. She wrote : " I think it would be better, and more striking to the reader, if you did not know either the name or the history of the subject.

"She was born near Geneva at 6 p.m. on 17th February, 1877. She had a rich and predestined life and died in Africa in 1904. I hope my idea is possible ; it would add greatly to the interest of the book and would silence all scoffers."

Astrologer's Letter to Correspondent

As will have been realised from earlier paragraphs, the writer does not specialise in " blind " astrology. Being busy at the time she did not feel inclined to take on this piece of work and began to write a letter which would explain this fully, which was necessary when refusing what had been a charmingly worded request.

It included the following :—

" Now, while I agree that, to a reader who has the usual somewhat crude idea of astrology, it might seem more striking if the work were done without any idea who the subject was, yet it might be perhaps better if it were done with a certain amount of ' case history ' which is the way all my work is done.

" The idea of the public about astrology is that it is a sort of fortune-telling and is therefore much cleverer of the astrologer if he knows nothing of the person he is writing about.

" In my own work, I treat the whole thing consultatively, seeing people and hearing their difficulties and trying to help them by means of their charts, just as the surgeon will advise through seeing the X-ray photograph.

" It seems to me that the public fails to realise (because it has never been told) that the birth-chart is not part of the person like the hand lines or the head bumps, but is an *astronomical* charting of the position of the ecliptic and planets in it at a specific moment of *time*.

The person or thing begun at that moment of *time* correlates forever with what is inherent in that *moment of time*. The interpretation of this is by means of the traditional symbolism and in broad lines would be the same for anybody born at that time and place. But, unless one has a certain amount of knowledge of the social status and conditions of life of the person, *it is impossible to word one's opinion suitably.*

" As an example, I was working yesterday on the chart of a clergyman. He had Venus rising in Pisces. Nothing more precisely expresses the idealistic and not very practical love for humanity which would press from the unconscious of a mentally brilliant man and urge him to give up academic distinction and become a parson. But suppose another life began at this same time and the child was born in squalid circumstances with no opportunity of mental development . . . this idealism and impracticality would probably get him no further than woolly actions and some longing for an absurd Utopia of the Communistic kind.

" As another example, suppose there was strong emphasis on the need for and ability to achieve happiness through partnership in life. A person whose fiancé was killed in a war might, through no fault of her own, never marry, thus never have children so that, while all the indication of ' urge ' was there, no remarks about husband and family would be applicable. Creativity might have all gone into artistic or literary work. Partnership might be satisfied by living with some great friend or going into business with someone.

" Thus, do you see, by a slightly inappropriate turn of speech, one might word a blind interpretation so that to the public it seemed all wrong ? "

Having written so far, a mood of inquisitiveness led to an examination of a quickly erected chart which at once seemed of real interest. Without elaborate note-making, as would be required for a full interpretation as usually given, a few comments were written on outstanding points asking whether these were of sufficient interest to proceed with the work.

Correspondent's Reply

Miss Blanch's immediate reply was galvanic (and again it must be remarked that it is difficult to give from personal experience, to try to show the rightness of astrological technique, without seeming to wish to sound as if saying " I was right " !) She wrote :—

" Your letter is *passionately interesting*. I am absolutely overwhelmed by the accuracy of your ' blind ' deductions. This should be a most remarkable example of astrological logic, a vindication if you like ! Can you do it in time ? Oh do try ! juggle with your other work ! I am spell-bound with interest now. Fact by fact what you say is correct. It is truly wonderful ! "

On her arrival in England, it was decided that, since space would be short, no expansion should be made, extracts from the original letter being published as written, except for minor editing by herself.* These are now reproduced with the addition of a few words from the original which are of interpretative interest but did not contribute to the story. Marginal significators and comment are added for the present readers.

* Isabelle Eberhardt " Portrait of a Legend " by Lesley Blanch, *The Cornhill Magazine*, **Spring**, 1952. Reproduced by kind permission of the Editor.

" MADEMOISELLE E " BY FORWARDS ASTROLOGY

Synthesis of significators †

Uranus, dispositor of Sun and of Mercury and Venus, rulers of Asc. and M.C. is in Leo, *very* strongly aspected and alone on eastern horizon. Saturn, ruler 5th (creative) in Pisces, in 7th Sun in Aquarius combining with Uranus, not only by opposition but by mutual reception.

Uranus, only planet near Asc. Venus, ruler M.C. in Aquarius in 6th. Sun in 6th, progressing through Pisces all her life.
Moon in Aries in 8th trine Mars. Planet in 7th is Saturn, unaspected except for semi-sextile Venus.

Neptune in 8th trine Jupiter.   Aquarius strongly tenanted with Uranus strongly aspected. Mars (con. Jupiter) trine Uranus (exact).
Neptune in 8th* closely aspecting Mercury, ruler, and Jupiter.   Five planets in water houses.

Sun and ruler in Aquarius.
Fire signs contain Uranus, (dispositor of Sun, Mercury and Venus) Moon, and the close Mars con. Jupiter.
Overstrong Mars (con. Jupiter) in 4th quincunx Pluto (exact).

Home (4th) indicated by Sag. containing Mars, trine Moon in sign of Mars, accentuated by Jupiter, ruler 4th.
Three sets of exact aspects, Uranus–Mars–Pluto, Mercury–Neptune and Saturn–Venus.
Saturn in 7th and ruler 5th but Leo (showmanship) strong through Uranus (as above) working behind the scenes (12th).
Mercury, Asc.-ruler square Neptune (exact).

Mercury, Asc-ruler and significator of mind and nerves square Neptune ; but strong Mars (con. Jupiter) aspecting Sun, Moon and Uranus.

Varying expression of Virgo and Leo with Uranus strong in Leo. Nearly all planets on west side ecliptic.
8th house strongly ruled and strongly tenanted.*

Astrological Postscript to a Biography

Here is a person of abundant creative force, with much sympathy, yet always a rebel, who must go her own way. A strongly individualistic nature.

There is something odd, or unusual in her appearance. Her relations with others are odd, too. She devotes herself to them and their " causes " with pugnacious intensity, yet she seems to be denied complete fulfilment herself.

She has great idealism and humanitarian instincts. An over-flowing, restless energy in an unusual way, connected with others. Yet, a mystical nature.

She has a way of standing alone in a detached manner when she wants to. While full of heart she seems to have brought some strain into her life, or suffered strain through over-sudden ridding herself of things and people she did not want.

She is a pioneer in foreign lands. She should have achieved some prominence.   If denied actual creativity in children, or a cause, she could be a remarkable actress.   She may have " taken the stage " in some other way.

There should be some special fragility of mind, of the nervous system, even though with a strong physique.

A person of alternate moods and much pride. A life, in a way in the hands of, or for, others. A very marked preoccupation with sex, death and the after-life.

* *Note.*—The writer feels that the old phrase for the 8th house, " the house of death," has obscured the full meaning that should be associated with a house which has, as its natural sign, Scorpio, the bodily correlatives of which are the generative organs. Hence *life* with all its sexual and creative fullness is emphasised as *death*, which is only a stage in life. Being the second from the seventh, all feelings shared with or engendered by others must be signified as well as possessions. The rulerships of Mars and Pluto both emphasise these ideas. Reference should be made to the keyword meaning given in the paragraph on the houses in Chapter 5.
† Note on Chart : In 4th house, for ♃ read ♂.

A few outstanding years at a glance	
Sun prog. con. Saturn	*Age 10–11* Something in the nature of a loss, a tragedy, a set-back.
Venus, by O-D, con. Sun	*Age 20* A great falling in love or other uniting happiness. A consumation, fulfilment.
Sun prog. (in 7th) aspecting Uranus Mars and Pluto, all in *exact* aspect at birth.	*Age 23–24* Sudden and unexpected changes. A crowded dramatic year of many events and dangers. Climax. Much to do with others ; possibly marriage.
Neptune, ruler 7th, in 8th and by O-D square Sun	*Age 27* Her death, apparently sudden, seems to have been more the fault of others than herself.

Much additional testimony could be given to the importance of these years, if full secondary directions and transits were to be added but the point of this particular section is to show how much can be deduced quickly from the known rate of progression of the Sun and from the use of the One-Degree measure.

As ever, the truth lies in the understanding of the true *principles* of the planets, their working through the signs and in the houses. If these are translated, as the use of the key-word system indicates, basic truth is arrived at and astrological technique is justified. In the opinion of the writer, astrology is better served by writing of *trends* in this manner, than by attempting to carry this further as exact statements of definite *events*. This can be done only by astrologers who add psychic ability or even strong intuitional powers to the rational deductions of astrology. Confirmation can now be made by backwards astrology, information being taken from the writings of the two authors mentioned.

ISABELLE EBERHARDT BY BACKWARDS ASTROLOGY

On meeting Lesley Blanch, it was interesting to hear that she was the wife of Romain Gary, French writer and diplomat, both enthusiastic travellers, writing vividly of their experiences. It was odd that, having spent months in tracing Isabelle Eberhardt through her fantastic life in North Africa and thinking her story the only one to be written, she should arrive in England to find a book on the same person just on the market !* Readers anxious to know more of so unusual a woman can get this from libraries.

Since Isabelle's activities were mainly in French Africa, she and her life and writings are better known in France than in England. Certainly the present writer had never heard of her so could not have connected her with " Mlle. E."

Such a character is so strange to our English outlook that it can only be explained by its racial inheritance, so different from anything to which we are accustomed.

Isabelle's mother was the wife of a rich and aristocratic Russian General. She ran off with her childrens' tutor, Trophimowsky, an ex-priest, brilliant, bitter and an eccentric nihilist. Isabelle was their child. The whole family background was bizarre, neurotic and with a suicidal strain.

At ten years of age (Sun to Saturn) the only stable person in the household, an elder sister, married a tradesman, shocking the aristocratic pride of the family. With her went the last semblance of order and tidiness in the house. Isabelle's sense of loss was profound.

* *The Destiny of Isabelle Eberhardt,* by Cicely Mackworth, Routledge & Kegan Paul, Ltd.

At twenty (Venus by O-D to conjunction Sun) she went to Algeria. She had a tremendous love-affair with an Arab, became a Moslem and may be said to have united herself for ever with Islam. Always having liked boys' clothes, she now dressed as an Arab man, lived a nomad life with the tribes in the deserts (the love of " playing a part "), usually in dire poverty and squalor. Returning to the coast, she worked at one time as a dock labourer (exaggerated strength of the Mars–Jupiter conjunction aspecting Sun and Moon). In all this odd behaviour and personal appearance as deduced, can be seen the working of Uranus, so strong in this map as already shown, driving her to freedom of every kind ; this combines with the effect of the exact square from Neptune in 8th to Mercury, her ruler.

Her intelligence was outstanding (Ruler of 3rd, Mars, placed in Sagittarius and conjunct Jupiter). She was a brilliant linguist and it was said that no one understood North Africa as she did.

She was an alcoholic and an opium taker ; she lived amongst Arabs in filth, disorder and danger yet she is remembered by her writings, first published in altered and distorted form after her death, then in 1922 the originals were found and with them publication was made so that much which was mysterious in her life was explained.

Now the full import of the Virgo Ascendant is seen. The writer feels that guessing at possible occupations of the owner of a chart is not good astrology so no such attempt had been made. A person with Virgo Ascendant may have any one of the many occupations which are *of the nature of* Virgo and Mercury. Looking backwards, it is correctly noted as suitable for one who was not only a writer but accustomed to making the most detailed and careful notes, and also was always on the move (Mercury).

It is interesting that since Mercury's closest aspect is an *exact* connection with Neptune, there is an undermining of the usual Virgo characteristics of cleanliness and love of hygiene, but Isabelle liked to improve the health of others and did much for the Arabs though completely neglecting herself. The connection is by square, called " bad " in older days of astrology. " Bad " or not, it is powerful because exact, and because Mercury is her ruler. The duality of Mercury is bemused into a dream, at one time sensual and at another mystical. The escapism of Neptune finds a path for itself in one or the other way of the 8th house.

Cecily Mackworth writes : " One may see in her an adventuress, an artist, a mystic, a warm human being who thought ill of no one ; loved the humblest and hated only that which was false and pretentious. She was all in turn. It is useless to look for a logical thread on which to hang so chaotic an existence. (Could there be a better phrase to describe the extremism of this exact Mercury–Neptune square !) Her life was a fantastic dream of liberty (Uranus). At least she had the courage (strong Mars) to live that dream to the end, accepting the misery and degradation that its realisation entailed, and proudly accepting death."

Isabelle herself used a Uranian phrase about herself, " I go my way alone."

A rebel from home and family, Islam stood for her as a symbol for both. She wanted to retire to its contemplative life and to live alone.

Arab mythology contains a long tradition of female marabouts who travelled the deserts disguised as men. Isabelle herself wondered whether she was being prepared for sainthood, or rather that unity with God which is the goal of Sufism. She kept these things to herself and her careful diary, showing the street-urchin side to the world. An Algerian priest wrote after her death " She drank more than any soldier in the Foreign Legion, smoked more *kif* than a hashish addict and made love for the pleasure of it " yet she wrote in her journal " God has sown fruitful seeds in my soul : complete detachment from the things of this world, faith, and a burning love, pitiful and infinite, for the suffering." (Uranian detachment with Virgo desire for service to others.)

At 23-24 (Sun p. aspecting Uranus, Mars and Pluto), she made her final break with her family, married an Arab clerk called Sliméne living with him in scandalous notoriety, yet always learning more and more of the Arabs whom she loved and putting what she knew into articles and stories, mainly for a journal called Akhbar, the Editor of which became, at that time, the most important influence in her life. The year was also remarkable for an attempt on her life.

In 1903, she met Lyautey, then a Colonel. After her death, he wrote : " She was what attracts me more than anything else, a rebel. What a joy to find someone who is truly herself, passing through life as freely as a bird through the air " (note the Uranian comparison with flying !). " I loved her for what she was and what she was not ! "

He saw that he could make use of her in sounding the opinion of the tribes as to his policy of peaceful penetration into dangerous parts of the desert and even in influencing them that their interest lay in accepting French protection. Isabelle rode through the desert on the pure-bred Arab horse which he had given her, happy but always living to extremes. Hardship had been too much for her. Her nerves (Mercury) and health gave way. Constant fever weakened her and she was obliged to submit to the unwelcome discipline of a hospital. She left it to join Sliméne in a crumbling hovel on the side of a deep gorge. Next morning, floods rushed down it in a rage of rapids and whirlpools from which few could be saved. Her body was found crushed beneath beams. No one knew whether she did try to leave the hut or whether she accepted calmly her last escape from life. There is a theory that Sliméne was by then revolted by her infidelities ; that he could have saved her but did not. As well as the easily seen One-Degree measure of Neptune square Sun which correlates with the mystery about her death, and the oddness of the fact that, though in the desert, she died of drowning, by reference to the ephemeris it may be seen that no less than three progressed planets were aspecting her Saturn in 7th (*was it Sliméne ?*)

These were Venus to the conjunction of Saturn progressed, Mars to the sextile and Mercury her ruler to the conjunction of Saturn radical. Also her Moon had progressed to its natal place in the 8th. For her, a new phase in life, even if by custom, it must be called death.

CHAPTER 13

INTERPRETATION OF NONAGESIMAL AND MIDHEAVEN

Chart J.—ALFRED, LORD TENNYSON

Reasons for inclusion

AFTER some years of intensive study of the bases on which the different systems of House Division rested, and of a comparison between the interpretations of planets in the resultant houses by various systems, the writer came to three conclusions.

Firstly, that with the growing importance of the northern regions of the world, it did not seem reasonable to shut one's eyes to the fact that charts erected by the systems of Campanus and Regiomontanus provided houses which became increasingly disproportionate in size as the given latitudes increased, becoming absurdly so after that of the arctic circle, while past that level, the system of Placidus did not provide the requisite for the intermediate house-cusps at all, since, where so many degrees of the ecliptic are circumpolar, these have no separate diurnal and nocturnal arcs, hence no semi-arcs to trisect, thus the basic requirement of the system is missing. These objections did not apply to the Equal House System.

Secondly, that by use of keyword meanings for planets, signs and houses so that short interpretation is not stretched to cover known facts, and furthermore by a rigid system of allotting marks to correctness of meaning for planets in comparing this, in one house or another, by the different systems, in charts of intimately known people, the results by the houses of the Equal House System were preferable to those by the others.

Thirdly, that an examination of old records showed that the Placidean system had been kept before the astrological public, not because of superior merit but because many years ago an industrious supporter had calculated and published Tables for all latitudes for its use, these being incorporated in the current ephemerides, and published thereafter by custom, there being practically no access to Tables by any other system so that comparison could be made.

Having come to these conclusions, the decision was made to widen the knowledge of students by teaching an understanding of *all* systems rather than one only, but to use the Equal House system* for all personal work.

Facing the problem

A problem arose immediately. Since the degree of ecliptic on the cusp of the 10th house was not now to be necessarily the same as that on the meridian (customarily called the Midheaven or the M.C.), and since both carried the meaning generally attributed by astrologers to the 10th house, analogous to the mode of expression of its natural sign Capricorn, what differentiation could be made ?

It is first necessary to realise that in the Equal House system the ecliptic itself is divided directly into twelve equal houses just as into twelve equal signs ; the house circles are not

_____

* For more detailed discussion, see *The Modern Text-book of Astrology* by the same author. Chapters 6 and 16.

BIRTH CHART

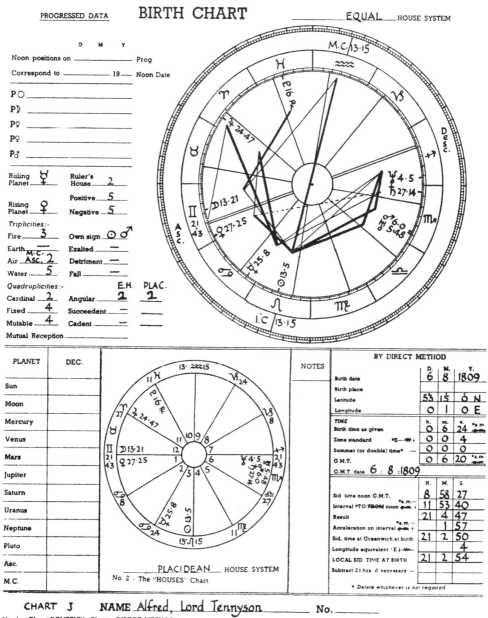

EQUAL HOUSE SYSTEM

Noon positions on _____ Prog

Correspond to _____ 19__ Noon Date

P ☉ _____
P ☽ _____
P ☿ _____
P ♀ _____
P ♂ _____

Ruling Planet ☿   Ruler's House 2

Rising Planet ♀   Positive 5
                   Negative 5

Triplicities:-
Fire 3   Own sign ☉ ♂
Earth —   Exalted —
Air ASC. 2   Detriment —
Water 5   Fall —

Quadruplicities:-   E.H. PLAC.
Cardinal 2   Angular   2   2
Fixed 4   Succeedent —   —
Mutable 4   Cadent   —   —

Mutual Reception _____

PLANET	DEC.
Sun	
Moon	
Mercury	
Venus	
Mars	
Jupiter	
Saturn	
Uranus	
Neptune	
Pluto	
Asc.	
M.C.	

PLACIDEAN HOUSE SYSTEM
No 2 - The "HOUSES" Chart.

NOTES

BY DIRECT METHOD

	D.	M.	Y.
Birth date	6	8	1809

Birth place			
Latitude	53	15	0 N
Longitude	0	1	0 E

TIME	h.	m.	s.
Birth time as given	0	6	24 *a.m.
Zone standard *E ÷ ₩ +	0	0	4
Summer (or double) time* —	0	0	0
G.M.T.	0	6	20 *a.m.

G.M.T. date 6 : 8 :1809

	H.	M.	S.
Sid time noon G.M.T.	8	58	27
Interval *TO/FROM noon *a.m.+	11	53	40
Result *a.m.—	21	4	47
Acceleration on interval *a.m. +		1	57
Sid. time at Greenwich at birth	21	2	50
Longitude equivalent *E ÷ ₩			4
LOCAL SID TIME AT BIRTH	21	2	54
Subtract 24 hrs. if necessary —			

* Delete whichever is not required

CHART J   NAME Alfred, Lord Tennyson _____ No. _____

No 1 The "ECLIPTIC" Chart. DIRECT METHOD

Designed by M.E.HONE.

dependent for their placing on the previous division of any other circle. Thus the quadruplicity represented by the sign containing the degree rising on the horizon (Ascendant) will also be represented by the sign containing the degree culminating at the meridian (Midheaven) and also by their two opposites. In this way (disregarding the rest of the chart for the moment) a person is deemed to be himself after his own manner according to the sign ascending ; and to express himself in the mode of the other signs of its quadruplicity in his outer life (10th) in his home life (4th) and in his close relationships with others (7th). From this grew the theory that *all people born with a certain sign ascending will express themselves in all the matters of the various houses in the sequential manner of the signs uniformly following on their cusps.* By the Equal House system, there can be no exaggerated enlargement of houses so that one, two or three signs are included in one house (interception) ; *the differences in expression being found by an examination of the conditioning of the rulers of those signs,* whether strong by angularity, by rulership, by aspect, by exaltation and so on.

Nonagesimal and Midheaven

The degree of the ecliptic on the cusp of the Equal House 10th house, being 90° from the degree on the horizon, and the highest point of the ecliptic from the horizon at any one time, is known astronomically as the nonagesimal. Since the sign of which it is a part is there *by natural order*, it became reasonable to suppose that a person would tend to express himself in the outer world, to realise his ambitions, and to gain his standing, in the mode of this sign since it would be his *natural* or innate manner of so doing.

The degree of the ecliptic on the cusp of the 10th house by the quadrant systems is that which is culminating at the meridian of the place in question. It is then at its greatest height from the horizon (but not necessarily the highest point of the ecliptic). The sign of which it is part, is there through the turning of the Earth on its axis in its daily rotation. It became equally reasonable to suppose that a person would express himself in the outer world, realise his ambitions and gain his standing in the world in the mode of this sign, if, in course of *time* (for this is a *time* factor), what has been called " the Earth impress " became more compulsive than his own innate predisposition.

For those born near the equator or in other latitudes with a sign rising which is not of extremely long or short ascension, the same sign would be on nonagesimal and midheaven. There would be no conflict between innate predisposition and the call or the push of what came to him on the stream of time.

For those having different signs on these two points, conflict must arise and there must be divided aspirations, *unless the rulers of these two signs are in happy relationship.* Interpretation of the expression through these signs must be by an examination and comparison of the strengths (by placing, aspecting and so on) of the two planets ruling them. The result of differing strengths will be shown by the hesitancy or alacrity with which the growing person seeks to express himself less or more as a natural human being according to his innate manner and similarly by the way in which he seeks to express himself as a citizen of his world, the events of which he must meet as a developing adult.

" A " and " M " Houses

From a prolonged consideration of these arguments, a theory arose in the London Astrological Research Group, of which the writer is a member, that, for full interpretation of a chart, *two sets of equal houses could be used in conjunction with each other.* Since by then the abbreviations Asc. and M.C. had been further shortened to A and M, the twelve houses following from the degree of the Asc. as cusp of the first house were called the A houses ; their house rulers and the planets in them being interpreted as showing *the innate predisposition of a person*, that is his character with deductions as to what he may be led to by it. The twelve following from the degree of M.C. as cusp of the 10th house, were called the M houses ; their house rulers and the planets in them being interpreted as showing *what he might have to meet and adapt himself to in life*, with deductions as to the way in which this could affect his character. A fuller description of this new theory can be read in the publication* of the Society but since there has not yet been time for it to be widely known, the example chart will be discussed only from the point of view of comparison of nonagesimal and midheaven.

Lord Tennyson, and his Outward Expression

Using the methods of backwards astrology, very necessary when trying to decide whether a theory has validity, it is known that Lord Tennyson was a writer, so the Gemini Ascendant is suitable. His nonagesimal, *and that of every other Geminian* is in Pisces.

Reference to a set of Tables of houses for northern latitudes shows that, while nearly all Geminians born in equatorial regions have Pisces on the meridian also, nearly all born in medium latitudes have a degree of Aquarius culminating while some of those born further north have Capricorn in that position.

This does bear out a generalisation that the average writer from southern climes will express himself in talking or writing in a more sentimental and feelingful way than, let us say, a London writer, while the Scot who writes and thinks, has a reputation for doing so in an even more hard-headed and practical manner.

Tennyson was a Geminian from the medium latitudes of our country, therefore likely to be the usual writer, author, journalist or teacher. Why was it that he concentrated on poetry and why did he become Poet Laureate when he did ?

This cannot be seen from an examination of nonagesimal and meridian alone. We must examine basically first. *All Geminians* in our latitudes, if the hypothesis is right, must *innately* desire to express themselves in the outer world in the Piscean mode. This they will do by the subtle means of bringing out, in the Geminian manner (communicative, versatile) that which is hidden, that which they get intuitionally. They must sympathetically enter into the feelings of others. This *may* be ethically done as by the subject of the present study but the " spiv " type of Geminian does it just the same. To sympathise means literally to *feel with*, thus the unethical but quick-minded person is able to " feel with " the public in sensing what it wants and selling it for his own profit. There is a Piscean escapism in any imaginative work of writing or painting, or the ways of quick-sale activity, whether all this is of a high or low standard.

A Geminian can write, think, paint or study in Piscean seclusion but the time comes when he realises that if his outer self-expression is to be recognised in the world and made lucrative, he must adapt himself to its requirements.

Leo is the sign of the heart. Its opposite, Aquarius, is that of the circulatory system. So, with Aquarius on the M.C., the Geminian of our latitudes must *circulate* both himself and the products of his brain or hands. *How* and *when* he will do this must depend on other factors in each individual chart.

Returning to Tennyson, it is known that he was able to write what was popular in his day since he sensed what the public wanted. He and his immediate contemporaries who

---

A and M houses, Transaction No. 1 of the London Astrological Research Group. To be obtained from Fowler & Co., 1201/1203 High Road, Chadwell Heath, Romford RM6 4DH, Essex.

were Geminian all had Uranus, *the ruler of the sign on the meridian*, in Scorpio, since it was in that sign for seven years. This may be one reason for much of the mystical, emotional writing at the time that these grew up.

Tennyson's Sun is in Leo. It is practically coincident with the lower meridian since he was born within a few minutes of midnight. The time given is 0.6.24 a.m. but this does not mean that the time of birth was so accurately taken. In *Notable Nativities** reference is given to a volume of *Modern Astrology* but this in turn quotes a second reference in N.N., this being to a magazine called *The Future*.†

In volume I, on page 55, the remark is made that the poet, in writing to an American critic whose book was published in 1891 said that he believed he was born " just after midnight " on 6th August. The Editor of the magazine, A. J. Pearce, states that he rectified the map to the published time by events in the life. For the present purpose, such exactitude does not matter, the important point being that the Sun is *trine* the ruler of the nonagesimal but *square* the ruler of the M.C. (wide aspect).

For this reason, the strong egotism of a Leo Sun (square Mars) would then find an easier path towards the *natural* expression of Pisces rather than the harder way of Aquarius.

For him, Mercury is not only the significator of the mind but is his Ascendant-ruler. It too is trine to Neptune, showing his second easy path to the Piscean way of expression. Neptune (ruler nonagesimal) has Saturn in conjunction but this, especially in Sagittarius (publishing) and with the trine to Mercury was probably a good stiffener against vagueness through the impressionability of Neptune.

Uranus (ruler M.C.) is much less well placed. It is conjunct Mars and square the Sun. Tennyson's tendency in life would then be towards his innate predisposition rather than towards what was to come to him on the stream of time. He himself wrote " the ideal which governs the lives of men, the eternal pattern which they seek *in time* to realise." Does his life-story uphold the theory of the interpretation of this pattern ?

Points from the Life Story Relevant to the Theory

A good ready-made character-study is necessary for this backwards‡ type of work so *Alfred Tennyson*,‖ by his grandson Charles Tennyson, was taken. What follows is not intended to be a complete interpretation but a selection of points to illustrate the interpretation of nonagesimal and midheaven.

Venus, ruler 5th (creativity) is conjunct the Ascendant, inclining his communicative Geminianism to a harmonious and beautiful expression, but the exact quincunx to Saturn would give it morbidity. (There is a story of one of his brothers introducing himself by saying " I am Septimus, the most morbid of all the Tennysons " !)

The Moon near an angle is said to give imaginative ability (see *Encyclopaedia of Psychological Astrology*, C. E. O. Carter), while Neptune, planet of boundlessness and imagination is in the 6th house, showing the *way* of his work to be of that order. As it is closely semi-sextile Uranus and Mars, the latter being ruler of the 6th house, health difficulties would be suspected and we read of his constant " nerves " and complaints about the functioning of his digestive and eliminative system (Moon square Pluto ?)

His mental slant is Leonian (Leo in 3rd), giving, as to all Geminians, a *power* over words, strengthened in his case by aspects to the Sun. Mercury is well connected to the

---

* *Notable Nativities*, Alan Leo's Astrological Manuals, L. N. Fowler & Co. Ltd.

† *The Future*, edited by A. J. Pearce.

‡ See Chapter 1.

‖ *Alfred Tennyson*, by his grandson, Charles Tennyson, 1949, Macmillan & Co.

planets in the 6th and is in the 2nd (money by Mercurial pursuits). The square to Jupiter is a good significator of the superabundant flow of words, made poetical by the Venusian and Neptunian contacts mentioned. To the writer, the glamour of his imagery is one of the earliest of memories, the verse about " an arm, clothed in white samite, mystic, wonderful," being one of the first to be learnt. It was therefore, something of a shock to read of the less admirable side of Neptune, so strong in the family background. All maps are " subsumed " (see *An Introduction to Political Astrology*, C. E. O. Carter, page 13), to others, personal maps to family maps. Here was a family of culture and knowledge, yet shiftless, impecunious and untidy. The father drank, two brothers were at times in mental homes, another became an opium addict. Alfred was moody when he could have been enjoying himself in company (Uranus conjunct Mars in Scorpio in 5th).

He seems to have used his powerful Sun to resist " the Earth impress " of Aquarius by every possible means, retiring in Piscean manner, to the isolation of his father's house in the country, even losing his little capital in a Neptunian " bubble scheme." In this he followed his innate inclination, desiring to be alone, like any writer who knows he must allow his unconscious self (12th house and Pisces) to have its way in peace.

Further evidence of inclination towards the things of Neptune is shown in his interest in psychic matters, he being a founder member of the Society for Psychical Research.

The change in his life came through the writing of the Poem *In Memoriam*. In his Piscean manner of behaviour in the world, he published this anonymously, but the force of the Aquarian M.C. began, in a subtle way, to overpower his reticence. Publishing it at his own risk, he himself took care of the business arrangements, that is, the preparation for its *circulation*. His biographer says this change of policy was evidence of his increased self-confidence ; he also says the poem represented an important stage in his struggle to find a *scientific* (Aquarian) basis for his beliefs and that he became most interested in the science of his day. Astrologers will like to hear that, later on, his interest in astronomy caused him to have a platform built from which to watch the stars, one of his sons being named Lionel because, at his birth, he was watching Mars culminating in Leo.

Now came a stroke of the good fortune hinted at by Jupiter, ruler 7th, in 11th, sextile Ascendant. Influential friends (11th) secured for him a pension from the Civil List. Objections to his marriage (7th) were withdrawn and the Poet Laureate died five weeks before the publication of the great poem. The obvious choice of successor was Samuel Rogers but he refused on account of his great age. Elizabeth Browning and Leigh Hunt were proposed, but *In Memoriam* swept London as a new musical play does now and one of its greatest admirers was the Prince Consort. He made inquiries about the author and, to Tennyson's great surprise, offered him the position.

It is not the purpose of this chapter to find from the chart a succession of aspects to match events in his life as dated by his biographers, but with the word " circulation " in mind for his sudden adoption of a life more in keeping with his Aquarian M.C., it is interesting to note that within the twelve months of his 42nd year, not only did his writings circulate everywhere but he himself was said to " step into a *round* of social life, including the Queen's Levee." Marriage, fame, money and social recognition came all at once.

Exact aspects in a natal chart denote very definite character-traits of the natures of the planets so combined. As life goes on, outstanding periods are to be expected when these are emphasised by directions or transits since the effect will always be dual. In the chart of this notable man there are no less than four such combinations ; Jupiter and Mercury, Sun and Moon (with M.C. and I.C. if correct), Mars and Uranus, Saturn and Venus.

By the use of the One-Degree measure (in which the number of degrees equal to the age is added to all planets), it can be seen that by adding 42°, the factors of the Sun–Moon–M.C.–I.C. formation, all make aspects (of the " compulsive " rather than the " easy " kind) to the important Jupiter–Mercury pair. Jupiter is in the house of friends and ruler of the marriage house, while Mercury is in the house connected with money and ruler of the Ascendant. By the same measure, these two make respectively the quincunx and sextile to Uranus (ruler M.C.) with its close conjunction to Mars in the 5th (creative) house. By the same addition to the degree in which Neptune is placed, it becomes sextile to Pluto in Pisces in the 10th house. Using the keyword, can we say that, at this time, Tennyson " eliminated " much of the Neptunian and Piscean condition which had characterised his life up till then ?

A few years before, his friends had thought him broken in health and will-power. Now he was famous. His biographer uses the very phrase applicable for the discussion of this theory. He says " Marriage, *In Memoriam* and the Laureateship broke down the last of his defences against *the stream of life.** The days of musing and brooding were over. The Recluse of Somersby had become a National Institution." (Compare the phrase earlier in the chapter. " The call or push of what came to him on *the stream of time.*") In other words, he had gone into circulation as impelled by his Aquarian M.C. !

* Italics of this phrase added by present writer.

BIRTH CHART

PROGRESSED DATA   EQUAL HOUSE SYSTEM

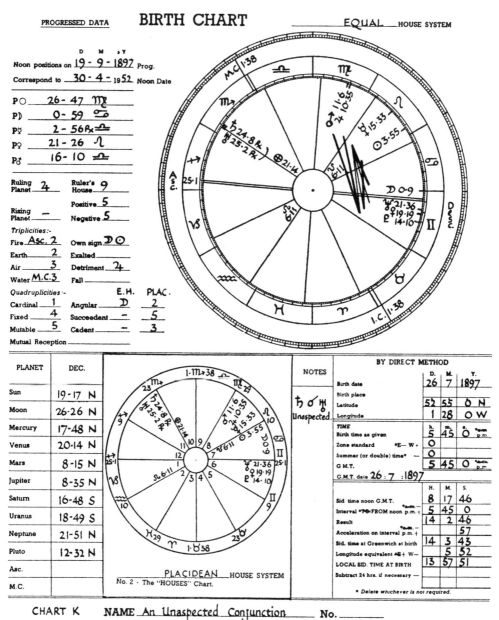

Noon positions on **19 - 9 - 1897** Prog.

Correspond to **30 - 4 - 1952** Noon Date

P☉	26 - 47	♍
P☽	0 - 59	♋
P☿	2 - 56 ℞	♎
P♀	21 - 26	♌
P♂	16 - 10	♎

Ruling Planet **4**   Ruler's House **9**

Rising Planet **—**   Positive **5**

     Negative **5**

Triplicities:-

Fire **Asc. 2**   Own sign **☽☉**

Earth **2**   Exalted

Air **3**   Detriment **4**

Water **M.C. 3**   Fall

Quadruplicities:-

           E.H.   PLAC.

Cardinal **1**   Angular **☽**   **2**

Fixed **4**   Succeedent **—**   **5**

Mutable **5**   Cadent **—**   **3**

Mutual Reception _____

PLANET	DEC.
Sun	19-17 N
Moon	26·26 N
Mercury	17·48 N
Venus	20·14 N
Mars	8-15 N
Jupiter	8-35 N
Saturn	16-48 S
Uranus	18-49 S
Neptune	21-51 N
Pluto	12-32 N
Asc.	
M.C.	

PLACIDEAN HOUSE SYSTEM

No. 2 - The "HOUSES" Chart.

NOTES

♄ ♂ ♅

Unaspected.

BY DIRECT METHOD

	D.	M.	Y.
Birth date	26	7	1897

Birth place

Latitude	52	55	0 N
Longitude	1	28	0 W

TIME

	h.	m.	s.	
Birth time as given	5	45	0	p.m.
Zone standard •E— W+	0			
Summer (or double) time* —	0			
G.M.T.	5	45	0	p.m.

G.M.T. date **26 : 7 : 1897**

	H.	M.	S.
Sid time noon G.M.T.	8	17	46
Interval TO/FROM noon p.m. †	5	45	0
Result	14	2	46
Acceleration on interval p.m. †			57
Sid. time at Greenwich at birth	14	3	43
Longitude equivalent •E + W—		5	52
LOCAL SID. TIME AT BIRTH	13	57	51
Subtract 24 hrs. if necessary —			

* Delete whichever is not required.

CHART K   NAME **An Unaspected Conjunction**   No. _____

No I   The "ECLIPTIC" Chart. DIRECT METHOD   Designed by M.E. HONE.

CHAPTER 14

INTERPRETATION OF UNASPECTED PLANETS

Chart K.—An Unaspected Conjunction

Reason for Inclusion

THIS point in interpretation has received little attention in the past. The unaspected planet has sometimes been alluded to as " a dumb note." The writer has formed the habit of listing all charts with a planet or planets in the comparatively rare state of having no aspects or having only a very wide minor aspect. The conclusion arrived at after some years of watchfulness is that a lone planet is by no means a dumb note. Its strength can be assessed in the usual ways, it being strong if it is Asc.-ruler or Sun-ruler, if conjunct the Asc. or M.C. or their opposites (on either side of the degrees occupied by these four points),* if dispositor of a satellitium, if in its own sign or the sign of its exaltation.

But, however, if without aspects, *the life-principle which is expressed by the planet, its urge or drive, will not easily be integrated with the other planetary principles in the personality.*

That which it represents, according to modification by placing in sign and house, will at times act entirely by itself without the helpful blending or controlling of other principles.

Like others of the finer points of astrological reasoning, this one is not easy to grasp if it is thought of as nothing more than an *astrological* factor in a chart. As soon as the *astronomical* basis is considered, it is possible to visualise a life, or anything else, making its beginning at a moment of a certain *pattern of time* because it is *of the nature of* that special pattern of time. If " Ecliptic " charts are used instead of " Houses " charts (using any system of house division) then the planets are spaced around the circle exactly as they truly are in the heavens at any given moment. This is the exact picture. Any house boundaries can be added since these are according to whatever system of house division is fancied. Lines can then be drawn between planets showing their angular relationships in their exactitude. *If these are thought of, not merely as a way of registering aspects, but as lines of expression from one planet to another*, it will be seen that, as in radar, such lines *radiating from a planet in all directions*, do not result in a " reflected wave " unless one falls on something which causes an answering response.

Such an answering response is part of the life-pattern of any person or thing begun at any moment with which its pattern is aligned. For this reason there is again response when time-sequences, later on, are of similar pattern, this perhaps being the rationale of the known effects of aspects made by planets by progression or transit to any pattern-point (occupied degree in natal chart) which is thus sensitised for such purpose.

When aspect lines are used, the isolation of the lone planet or the lone pair of planets, or the lone set of planets related to each other but not to the planets forming another set in the chart, is immediately seen.

---

* Ptolemy said that planets are strong *when near an angle*. It is only a development of this to call *houses* " angular, succedent and cadent." This over-emphasis on house position and this nomenclature has led to the irrational idea that if for example two planets are in close conjunction with each other being equidistant from the M.C., the one which is a few degrees east of the M.C. is strong because it is in an " angular " house while the western one is weak because it is in a " cadent " house.

Venus and Mercury are comparatively often thus short of aspects since they cannot be far from the Sun but are often just far enough not to make any aspect to it or to each other. In such cases, the Venusian urge to unison in affection with others or to possessiveness with material things is not necessarily lacking unless the planet is weakly placed but seems to be without means of expression, thus being apt to try to act, at times, by itself without the influence of mind and control. From the lone but well placed Mercury, deductions can be drawn of mental and nervous strength but there will be times in the life when the mental attitude does not seem to blend with the emotions, or a physical result may occur in that the movements of the hands are vague or unrestrained.

When two or more planets are closely interlinked but cut off from other planets by receiving no aspects from them, there can be what amounts to a split in the personality.

In astrological interpretation, the word " integration " is used in different senses by different workers. The present writer puts forward the idea that *integration in a personality may be judged by the interplanetary angular relationships.* Of these, the more the better, whether of the easy or the compulsive variety, each being considered as *an avenue of expression and impression for the self.*

In the case of two planets being, for instance, in conjunction with or in square or trine to each other but not aspecting any other planet (or having only very minor aspects from others) great care and tact must be used in any " blind " interpretations. The split may indeed be sufficiently severe to cause some division in the personality but such a suggestion might be deeply wounding to the person concerned and better left without comment. In the case of an interview, some explanation may be offered by the client if an opportunity is given.

On one occasion when studying such a map (Mars square Neptune with no other aspectual links) the information was given by its owner that his imbalance had led to a breakdown after a crisis in life, after which for some years he had not been the same again. During the worst of his illness he had suffered abnormally from insomnia which had ruined his nerves. He himself used the phrase that he had begun to live " almost a Jekyll and Hyde kind of life." There was also a curious effect that he could not properly see red, the colour of Mars, and had to allow for this when driving and noticing traffic lights.

Another case will show that in a strong map, the unintegrated part of the personality may be used separately for a purpose correlative with the nature of the unaspected planet, which though good, may have the effect of separating one side of the life from the rest. Here, an unaspected Jupiter in the 8th house seemed to agree with strength of deeper emotions but also with a need to find " expansion " in life through distant travel, the man being cut off from all ordinary life for long periods of time spent in work in Antarctic regions.

In another case of an unaspected Mars (in Aries) its strength was noticeable in the life but with times of unrelatedness to the rest of the personality. The man in whose chart this occurred had some understanding of astrology and felt that this theory was the first which gave him a true understanding of himself. He said that his tempers were " like a flash of lightning and uncontrollable *as if apart from him.*" In such moods, he could easily think of murder. Then, as suddenly, a calm would follow. He also had difficulty with the colour red, not being able to match shades of it properly.

Chart of an Unaspected Conjunction

This chart is chosen for inclusion because it so perfectly exemplifies the point. The writer was at first perplexed as to the possible meaning of the unaspected conjunction of Uranus and Saturn. When unsure, the more basic the interpretation the more near to the truth it is likely to be. In the short interpretative paragraphs on aspects in *The Modern*

Text-book of Astrology, the attempt was made to write these as nearly as possible in accordance with straightforward keyword meanings in combination. Thus the paragraph on this conjunction was brought into the short notes which were made by forwards astrology, not for a full interpretation but for a talk about the chart with its unknown owner. Extracts relevant to the point now raised were as follows :—

Significators	*Notes*
Ruler con. Mars ; Sun in Leo No helpful aspects to either	An interesting chart since it shows a life which is basically strong and powerful, yet cannot find easy channels for personal expression and fails to be truly integrated.
Uranus con. Saturn, otherwise unaspected	A man with a distinct split in his personality.
The lone conjunction in Scorpio Conjunction on 12th cusp	He has to try to combine self-will with self-control in his emotional life and this is not easy. However, though this may set up a nervous tension, it may produce some practical planning with unusual results or in an unusual way, perhaps not altogether public.
Nonagesimal Virgo, strengthened by Mars and Jupiter	The tendency of his character is to do something which is energetically practical.
M.C. Scorpio (see Chapter 13)	Probable development is more towards investigatory interests.

On meeting the owner of the chart, it appeared that he had not adopted any profession in accordance with his Sagittarian Ascendant (though he was a lover of dogs) but had followed the urge of his nonagesimal and its ruler Mercury. In this case, his path was shown as an easy one in the chart since the sign in which it was, contained also his ruler, it being pressed to activity by the conjunction of Mars, while Mercury was the best aspected planet linking by sextile with Venus, Neptune and Pluto in the 6th. Mercurial ability had been used by the energetic work of his hands and mind in art. He had used all media, had made teaching his life-work and excelled at craft-work. He also used his hands for healing.

On hearing the meaning of the lone conjunction, he offered the explanation that the short phrases of the notes were indeed tragically true ; that " *so keenly had I felt the split in my nature that at times I had seemed as if about to disintegrate into a nothingness, without even the relief of going mad.*"

But there was another side to the story. As also indicated by the notes, he had *used* this part of himself in a planned activity of a most unusual nature and very definitely in a non-public way. He had developed a curious separation of the self in which he could sit quietly with anyone bereaved and allow one side of himself to become aware of the personality of the dear one who had died. He could then paint a portrait of him as clearly as if he had been there. Whether this was by means of spirit help or by telepathy from the visitor he did not know.

Later remarks made by him showed how closely this conjunction was true in accepted astrological reasoning. Uranus is the ruler of his 3rd house (by Equal House system) and thus the significator of his mental attitude and reactions. Here it is, limited, or one might also say concentrated by its one aspect with Saturn, so his own phrase was " Often, I felt I couldn't even *see* a joke nor did I want to laugh about things, I felt so sad."

In regard to the difficult aspects to ruler and to Sun, he said he was very conscious of the difficulty in using his powers and abilities, so that, whatever he did, every avenue of expression always seemed blocked. He could get so far and no farther.

Teaching finally came to an end, after which occurred a time of *mental numbness*, this being very like what happened in the first case mentioned. He said " *Concentration* was *disrupted* and life seemed *divided*." Note the use of words exactly applicable to the two planets and to the theory brought forward in this chapter.

Later on, he had come to an activity consonant with the investigatory side of Scorpio, the sign on his M.C., since he had become a keen researcher into psychic matters.

CHAPTER 15

INTERPRETATION OF INCEPTIONAL MAPS

Charts L and M.—A TEACHER OF ASTROLOGY AND THE MOMENT OF HER FIRST CLASS

Reason for Inclusion

As the natal chart is my own, and since one glance at it will show that it has a Leo Ascendant, it is just as well to be preposterously Leo at this point and to say that this inceptional chart is included because it is the best I know ! ! ! Needless to say, all such charts will not be so amazingly mirror-like in their reflection of the matter begun at a given moment, nor will all so equally amazingly fit with the chart of the person making the beginning, but in this book an attempt is being made to show that astrology truly *is* amazing to those who watch the disclosing of the hidden pattern of which it is an interpretation. Again, apology must be made for being personal, but how else can factual experience be given for the use of others ? One is reminded of Alan Leo who is said to have remarked that work was everything and work meant cleansing the Augean stables of astrology and founding a modern system which others could follow. To him, the doer of the work meant nothing. " Don't think of Alan Leo " he often said, " think of the work that is given to him to do." Perhaps another Leo with the same ascending degree may be forgiven for being personal when trying to help to carry on the perpetual modernising of astrology which has always been a necessity in each period for some few thousands of years !

There is no privacy about my own chart as it has been used as an example in teaching for many years so can now be used as a basis for this chapter on the interpretation of *Inceptional Charts*.

Confusion is sometimes made between these and *Electional Charts*. These are charts of moments carefully chosen so that a matter to be begun may have the best possible beginning. *Inceptional Charts* are of moments when something of importance actually did begin, the time being taken and the map examined.

The Inceptional Moment

After many years of study and some experience of private teaching, it was decided that I should for the first time take a formal class in a room in London engaged for the purpose. It had to be at 6.30 p.m. B.S.T. to suit some members who were working and could not come earlier. This having been decided upon and announced, the map was drawn. So extraordinarily did it fit the occasion that every care was taken to see that the class began promptly at that time.

As mere humans, we cannot be expected to understand the universal pattern. A daffodil cannot understand why its blooming smoothly fits in with a moment in spring. Fish which journey to their breeding places cannot understand how it is that they instinctively align themselves with the time factor as they do so. A study of inceptional maps shows that human beings do seem to fit their actions (which they think they do by free will) to moments of time so that they, like daffodils and fishes, play their appointed parts in the perpetual drama as it unfolds. The moments decided upon for the launching of ships which have been lost provide charts worth study in this respect.

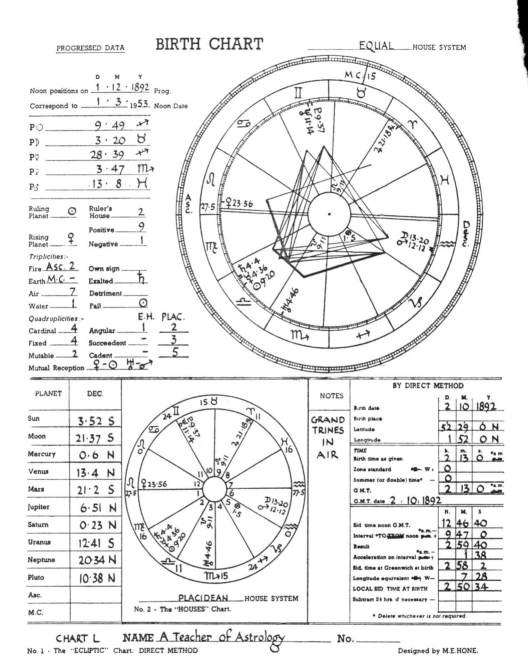

PROGRESSED DATA   **BIRTH CHART**   EQUAL HOUSE SYSTEM

M.C. 15

	D	M	Y	
Noon positions on	1	12	1892	Prog.
Correspond to	1	3	1953	Noon Date

P☉   9 · 49 ♐
P☽   3 · 20 ♉
P☿   28 · 39 ♐
P♃   3 · 47 ♏
P♂   13 · 8 ♓

Ruling Planet	☉	Ruler's House	2
		Positive	9
Rising Planet	♀	Negative	1

Triplicities:-
Fire Asc. 2   Own sign ___
Earth M.C. -   Exalted ♄
Air 7   Detriment ___
Water 1   Fall ☉

Quadruplicities:-
			E.H.	PLAC.
Cardinal	4	Angular	1	2
Fixed	4	Succeedent	-	3
Mutable	2	Cadent	-	5

Mutual Reception ♀ - ☉ ♅ - ♂

PLANET	DEC.
Sun	3·52 S
Moon	21·37 S
Mercury	0·6 N
Venus	13·4 N
Mars	21·2 S
Jupiter	6·51 N
Saturn	0·23 N
Uranus	12·41 S
Neptune	20·34 N
Pluto	10·38 N
Asc.	
M.C.	

NOTES

GRAND TRINES IN AIR

PLACIDEAN HOUSE SYSTEM
No. 2 - The "HOUSES" Chart.

BY DIRECT METHOD

	D.	M.	Y.
Birth date	2	10	1892
Birth place			
Latitude	52	29	6 N
Longitude	1	52	0 N

TIME		m.	s.	
Birth time as given	2	13	0	a.m.
Zone standard W +	0			
Summer (or double) time*	0			
G.M.T.	2	13	0	a.m.

G.M.T. date 2 : 10 : 1892

	H.	M.	S
Sid time noon G.M.T.	12	46	40
Interval *TO FROM noon a.m. +	9	47	0
Result	2	59	40
Acceleration on interval a.m. +		1	38
Sid. time at Greenwich at birth	2	58	2
Longitude equivalent W—		7	28
LOCAL SID TIME AT BIRTH	2	50	34

Subtract 24 hrs. if necessary —

* Delete whichever is not required.

CHART L   NAME A Teacher of Astrology   No._____
No. 1 - The "ECLIPTIC" Chart. DIRECT METHOD   Designed by M.E.HONE.

Special Factors in Chart	Interpretation
Virgo rising	Detailed work of teaching, critical attitude.
Gemini culminating with satellitium in that sign.	Tuitional work in the outer world, strongly emphasised.
Ruler, Mercury, in Aquarius in 6th square Uranus.	Planet of mental communicative work, in the house of work, in the sign under which astrology is usually placed, stressfully and compulsorily connected with planet of astrology.
Sun in Pisces in 7th. Mutual reception with Jupiter.	Intuition used as well as mind. Necessity for increasing work with others.
Mercury, ruler, in 27° Aquarius. Sun, in 11° Pisces	The chart is suitable for the work, since these two most important planets are in *the two degrees* mentioned by Charles Carter* as associated with astrology.
Uranus conjunct M.C. and in mutual reception with ruler, Mercury	Work is Uranian, under which category astrology is usually placed. Outer self expression and mental work in an unusual subject go well together.
Sun and Uranus closely conjunct angles	Strength shown in the vitality of the enterprise and the astrological career.
All planets strongly aspected	Plenty of lines of expression.
Unusual satellitium around M.C. (unusual since not formed by Sun, Mercury, Venus)	Strong activity out in the world, not at home.
Exact semi-sextile between Sun and Venus, and between Saturn and Jupiter. (Sun is square to mid-point of satellitium and Venus is trine to it)	A fine counterbalance in affairs since a " difficult " or compulsive aspect by progression, one-degree measure or transit from one planet will usually be accompanied by a " helpful " one from the other.
Sun, ruler 12th in 7th squares satellitium at M.C.	That which is hidden in knowledge is brought to others and put over to the public but by hard work and with many difficulties.
Venus in Aquarius in 6th trine satellitium	Much happiness in the work, many friendships resulting from it.
Moon in Gemini conjunct Uranus	Expression through talking, teaching and writing of astrology.
Mars conjunct Saturn in 10th but trine Venus and sextile Jupiter as well as square Sun	Hard ambitious work, tiring but bringing opportunities and contentedness.
Neptune (ruler 7th and Sun-ruler), strongly aspected in 1st, forming grand trine with Venus (in Aquarius in 6th) Uranus and Moon in Gemini at M.C.	Idealism for work of astrology taught to the public.

* *Encyclopædia of Psychological Astrology*, 3rd Edition, page 40, by C. E. O. Carter.

BIRTH CHART

PROGRESSED DATA　　　　　　　　　　　EQUAL HOUSE SYSTEM

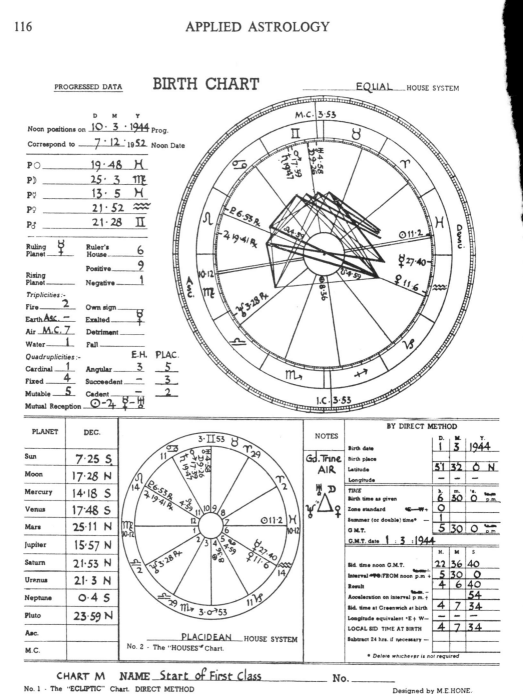

	D	M	Y
Noon positions on	10 · 3 · 1944 Prog.		
Correspond to	7 · 12 · 1952 Noon Date		

P☉ ___ 19·48 ♓
P☽ ___ 25·3 ♍
P☿ ___ 13·5 ♓
P♀ ___ 21·52 ♒
P♂ ___ 21·28 ♊

Ruling Planet	♅	Ruler's House	6
		Positive	9
Rising Planet		Negative	1

Triplicities :-
Fire __ 2 ___ Own sign ___
Earth __ Asc. ─ ___ Exalted ♅
Air __ M.C. 7 ___ Detriment ___
Water __ 1 ___ Fall ___

Quadruplicities :-　　　　　E.H.　PLAC.
Cardinal __ 1 ___ Angular __ 3 ___ 5
Fixed __ 4 ___ Succeedent __ ─ ___ 3
Mutable __ 5 ___ Cadent __ ─ ___ 2
Mutual Reception ☉-♃ ♅-♅

M.C. 3·53

I.C. 3·53

PLANET	DEC.
Sun	7·25 S
Moon	17·28 N
Mercury	14·18 S
Venus	17·48 S
Mars	25·11 N
Jupiter	15·57 N
Saturn	21·53 N
Uranus	21·3 N
Neptune	0·4 S
Pluto	23·59 N
Asc.	
M.C.	

NOTES

Gd. Trine AIR

♅ ☽
♃ △ ♀

3·II 53

No. 2 - The "HOUSES" Chart.

PLACIDEAN HOUSE SYSTEM

BY DIRECT METHOD

	D.	M.	Y.
Birth date	1	3	1944
Birth place			
Latitude	51	32	0 N
Longitude	─	─	─

TIME	h.	m.	s.
Birth time as given	6	30	0 p.m.
Zone standard ←E→ +W+	0		
Summer (or double) time*	1		
G.M.T.	5	30	0 p.m.

G.M.T. date 1 : 3 : 1944

	H.	M	S
Sid. time noon G.M.T.	22	36	40
Interval →TO/FROM noon p.m +	5	30	0
Result	4	6	40
Acceleration on interval p m. +			54
Sid. time at Greenwich at birth	4	7	34
Longitude equivalent *E + W─	─	─	─
LOCAL SID TIME AT BIRTH	4	7	34
Subtract 24 hrs. if necessary ─			

* Delete whichever is not required

CHART M　NAME Start of First Class　　　　No. _____

No. 1 - The "ECLIPTIC" Chart. DIRECT METHOD

Designed by M.E.HONE.

Comment

It would seem to be impossible to have made up a chart or even picked out a moment which could so effectively have portrayed the matter to be begun. A general assessment shows further unusual features in that there are *seven* planets in Air signs, suitable for mental work, four of these and the M.C. being in a *grand trine* which is well balanced by accompanying squares and oppositions so has no implication of laziness ; and that there are no less than *nine* of the ten planets in positive signs, implying self-expressive activity.

Personal Chart

A glance at the personal chart shows that this inceptional chart was for the work of one who also had the unusual number of *nine* planets in positive signs, *seven* again being in Air. Again there is a *grand trine*, the degrees occupied being almost identical with those in the inceptional chart ! 27° *Leo*, one of the degrees associated with astrology ascends. *Moon and Mars* mainly well aspected in 6th house in Aquarius show energetic work for the public in astrological ways. The close conjunction of *Saturn to Mercury* and the closeness of the progressed conjunction to *the Sun* for many years in middle life show the delay of much achievement until later years.

More personal interpretation may safely be left to readers.

Inceptional Map: its Planets being Considered as Transits

The planets of any inceptional map should be studied as *transits* of the moment to the map of the person concerned. In this case, the overlaying of the one grand trine by the other means that *all the four planets* in the one make close conjunctions and trines to *all the seven* in the other.

The ruler of the inceptional is conjunct the 7th cusp of the personal, showing that many others had to come into the life both as students and colleagues. Jupiter in the inceptional is trine to Jupiter in the personal.

Development of an Inceptional Chart

An inceptional map can be studied for time sequences as shown by progressions and transits. For instance, a chart for the moment of the beginning of married life, or for the start of a business company can be so used.

In relation to the present chart, by backwards astrology, it can be seen that appropriate developments in the teaching career can be fitted to planetary changes by customary methods of progression.

In the first four years, teaching was continued with constant effort to develop a system whereby the work of both tutor and student could be more methodical and straightforward. The next five years covered a period of fruition of experience thus gained, it being very remarkable that, during this time (as listed below) so many aspects in the chart became exact by progression. As can be seen by the data for the personal chart, the writer then reached her sixtieth birthday so it would not be likely that such a period of concentrated activity should recur at any other time.

Events and their Significators 1948–52

Significator	*Occurence*
1948 Mars p. closes conjunction to Saturn and sextile to Jupiter 1948–50. Mercury p. closes square to Uranus.	Start of teaching in new foundation of Faculty of Astrological Studies.

1949   Venus p. closes trine to Mars. Mercury p. quincunx Pluto. Mars p. conjunct Saturn p. Moon p. passes from conjunction Pluto to conjunction Jupiter, both in Leo.

New phase through election to senior offices in teaching with increased organisational work.

1950   Mars p. still close conjunction Saturn and sextile Jupiter

Hard work on *The Modern Text-book of Astrology*. Acceptance by publishers.

1951   Sun p. closes square to Mars. Venus " O-D " trine Mars. Venus (ruler 9th) closes trine Saturn opposition Jupiter.

Work difficult but happy. *Text-book* published towards end of year. At same time, tuition extended to many foreign countries through planning of Course for External Students of Faculty.

1952   Mercury p. (ruler) conjunct Sun. Venus (ruler 9th) trine progressed Mars

Applied Astrology written. Vigorous growth of new Course, especially abroad, making many new and happy personal contacts. Many lectures to various Societies.

An interesting point of interpretation is that, in this chart which is to do with work, involving close attention to duties, strong aspects are made to Saturn, these coming to exactitude in the years when the main work was done. The old word " malefic " was very unkind to Saturn, giving no credit to its nature as understood by the keyword " limitation." Work naturally brings responsibility and limitation, especially of *time*, of which Saturn is often taken as significator. Saturn has been called " The Reaper " ; it is noticeable that the autumn of 1951, was the time of results of years of preparation, culminating in the decision that the text-book (written as far as possible to cover Faculty policy regarding the basic concepts of astrology) should be used as the official text-book of the Faculty and that it should be the foundation on which the Course for External Students should be built. *This was the very period during which Saturn transited, by conjunction and trine, all the degrees of the grand trines of both the personal and the inceptional chart.*

Future Prospects

By forwards astrology, *trends* can be noted definitely, but though appropriate end-results of these may be suggested, detailed foreknowledge is not possible. During 1953, the Sun will close its square to Saturn, at the same time forming the quincunx to Jupiter. About three and a half years later Mercury, the ruler of the map will form the same aspects. " Father Time " will undoubtedly make his limitations felt and will impose his responsibilities. They are awaited with interest.